The Official

Nancy Barr

Dolly Parton Scrapbook

The Official Dolly Parton Scrapbook

by Connie Berman

Foreword by Dolly Parton

A TARGET BOOK
GROSSET & DUNLAP, INC., PUBLISHERS, NEW YORK, N.Y. 10010

Nancy Barr

Nancy Barr

Nancy Barr

The publisher gratefully acknowledges permission to use material from the following:

"What Would You Get If You Crossed Mae West with Norman Vincent Peale?" An interview with Dolly Parton by Chet Flippo. *Rolling Stone,* Issue #246, August 25, 1977.

An interview with Dolly Parton published in *Us Magazine* in 1978.

An article on Dolly Parton printed in *The Village Voice* on December 6, 1976. Reprinted by permission of *The Village Voice.* Copyright © The Village Voice, Inc. 1976.

Abridged from The Official Dolly Parton Scrapbook

Published simultaneously in Canada

Target ISBN: 0-448-15569-9

Printed in the United States of America

Contents

THIS BOOK IS FOR MY FANS — PRESENT AND FUTURE. I HAVE ALWAYS ENJOYED TRAVELLING AROUND THE COUNTRY PERFORMING FOR YOU AND IN RETURN FOR ALL THE JOY YOU'VE GIVEN ME, I WOULD LIKE TO GIVE YOU A CHANCE TO GET TO KNOW ME BETTER BOTH AS A PERSON AND MY LIFE ON THE ROAD. I WISH I COULD MEET ALL OF YOU IN PERSON BUT I KNOW THAT'S NOT POSSIBLE. I JUST WANT YOU TO KNOW THAT...

I HOPE LIFE TREATS YOU KIND.
I HOPE YOU HAVE ALL YOU EVER DREAMED OF.
I WISH YOU JOY AND HAPPINESS,
BUT ABOVE ALL THIS
I WISH YOU LOVE.

Nancy Barr

Mike Borum

Introduction

She teeters on spiky, spindly high heels, her petite five-foot frame perched daintily. Her lush, well-endowed body with one of the most famous bustlines since Jane Russell is encased in a sequinned jumpsuit, clinging as tight as a second skin. Her dimpled smile is shimmering and radiant as she sings to the crowd. But the main thing you notice about Dolly Parton is her abundance of meringue-colored hair that curls around her pale-skinned face, a luminous nimbus of waves and twirls. It is a Nashville store-bought halo offsetting her face. Sweet Dolly from the Smoky Mountains in Tennessee is some sort of country angel, imported to save our sinning souls, or at least to grant us a bit of melodic respite from earthly pain.

If Dolly, with her towering platinum wigs and the outrageously slinky outfits that make Frederick of Hollywood's collections seem tame, appears larger than life, well, that's her aim. "I want to be a superstar. An international star. A universal star. I want to be everything I dream of bein' and I'm dreamin' big."

In an era where the ordinary man has been elevated to stardom, where the matinee idol tends to be short and squat and a bit rotund, where the Hollywood glamour girl can be gap-toothed and small-breasted with skinny legs, Dolly Parton has a refreshing old-fashioned brand of glittery charisma—the appeal of legends like Jean Harlow and Marilyn Monroe. Strangely dressed as she may be by today's sleek standards, Dolly Parton is a unique personality with her own style and mannerisms that nody can make her change.

Since 1964, when Dolly Parton first arrived in Nashville after high school graduation, she has won just about every award that the country-music industry bestows. For the past several years she has reigned as the Queen of Country, edging out such old-guard empresses as Loretta Lynn and Tammy Wynette. But even that did not keep a restless and ever-climbing soul like Dolly's content. In 1977, against the cautionary advice of some of the most respected country-music people, she set out to conquer pop audiences as well. Dolly was determined and she won out. She has become the first country performer effectively to cross that formidable demarcation line between country and pop, and is now well on her way to being one of the most important female entertainers of our time—as well as one of the most intriguing celebrities in the country, with her cotton-candy looks and her backwoods blend of innocence and shrewdness.

Today everybody—from hillbilly fan to urban

Dolly, lost in her dreams.

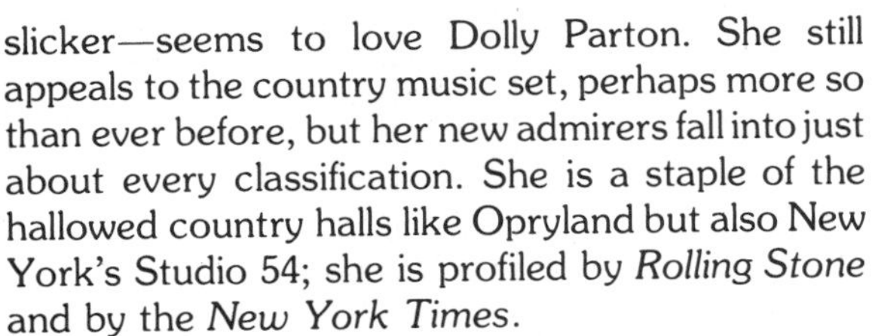

slicker—seems to love Dolly Parton. She still appeals to the country music set, perhaps more so than ever before, but her new admirers fall into just about every classification. She is a staple of the hallowed country halls like Opryland but also New York's Studio 54; she is profiled by *Rolling Stone* and by the *New York Times*.

If the pace of Dolly Parton's skyrocket to fame is surprising to observers, it is not surprising at all to her.

"Am I surprised I'm successful?" she asks, with a dimpled grin. "No. Actually I thought I'd be bigger than this. I just feel like I'm just startin' out. I know everything will be as I've been dreamin' it, because I got so many things I want to do. I know now that I'm just gettin' started for what I want to do. I expected this fame and I planned for it, so I know how to handle it real good."

She started planning for success as a child growing up dirt-poor in a wooden shack in Tennessee, spinning out songs and dreaming dreams that other mountain folk would have considered impossible tomfoolery. A spunky, determined kid, she cut a record before she was in her teens and talked her way into a singing appearance on the "Grand Ole Opry" show before she was out of high school.

After high school, Dolly headed straight for Nashville, where she pounded the pavements and came to prominence in 1967 when she became the new singing partner of Porter Wagoner. She decided to go solo in 1974 and, after a series of resounding successes, made the big leap into pop music in 1977, having hired a new band called Gypsy Fever. Now, as testimony to her success and widespread appeal, she has a major movie contract, and Dolly dolls sell by the thousands to her fans, as do her pinup wall posters.

But all this is according to the plan Dolly set forth for herself as a youngster when she had fantasies of lots of money and glamourous clothes and fancy houses and cars. She has all that today and more.

"I know who I am, where I'm going, what I want," Dolly says without a trace of doubt. It is obvious that she always knew. When she was growing up in the mountains, Dolly read fairy-tale stories. Now she is living out her own fairy tale, starring in it in platinum-blond color.

Dolly strikes a typically jubilant pose as she arrives at Heathrow Airport in London for the eighth International Festival of Country Music in 1976.

Wide World Photos

Nancy Barr

Mike Borum

Smoky Mountain Childhood

Sevier County, Tennessee, is the epitome of "country." To be sure, there are fancy fast-food places, sleek modern hostelries, and even newfangled discotheques that dot the main highway in the county. But, off on the side roads, just yards away from all these trendy monuments to 1970 culture, are clusters of tiny villages where the mountain folk live—and live plainly. Nestled away in the Smoky Mountains, these small hamlets seem untouched by contemporary civilization. These are places of fundamentalist religion, authentic log cabins, places where the front yards are mostly dirt or else taken up by vegetable patches and pecking chickens. Sometimes you'll see a local resident twanging a guitar (or some object fashioned into a makeshift string instrument) on his porch. These are places where a "foreigner" could be a stranger from the next town over, and people make their living mostly from the land.

Sevierville, in Sevier County, is one of these places. It is only two hundred miles east of Nashville, yet in some respects it is light years away. It is so small that you could pass right through it without realizing that you had gone through a town. There are towering pine trees, maples, and tobacco fields, and many of the names on the mailboxes are the same—a trademark of interrelated country life-style. The phone book for Sevier County, just 605 pages and including Sevierville, lists about 100 Partons, probably all some kind of relative to Dolly.

This is Dolly Parton's homeland, the place that nurtured her zealous determination to become a star and the place that she has so hauntingly immortalized in her poetic and evocative songs.

Dolly Rebecca Parton was born early on a snowy morning, January 19, 1946, in a wooden shack on the Little Pigeon River in Sevierville. Of Dutch, Irish, and Cherokee Indian ancestry, she was the fourth of twelve children of Avie Lee and Robert Lee Parton. Willadeene, David, and Denver came before; and afterwards were Bobby, Stella, Cassie, Randy, Larry (who died a few hours after birth), the twins Floyd and Frieda, and Rachel.

Her mother was just twenty-two—she had married at fifteen—when Dolly was born. "mama and daddy were just kids when they had kids," she likes to say. Her father worked at odd jobs—farming mostly—and the family struggled to make ends meet. Money was scarce, and sometimes the Partons had none at all. When Dolly was delivered, the doctor, Dr. Robert F. Thomas, was paid with a sack of flour.

Courtesy of Dolly Parton

Dolly's family in 1960. Standing, left to right: Randy, Dolly, Willadeene, Denver, Floyd, Bobby, Freida, and David. Seated, left to right: Stella, Dolly's mother Avie Lee, her father Robert Lee, and Cassie.

Dolly's childhood was humble, not only because the Partons lived in poverty but also because the family was pretty much isolated from big-city or even small-town life. There was no television, telephone, or automobile—just an old battery radio that tuned in and out. Dolly recalls that she and the rest of the Parton clan lived in their two-room home up in the mountains, hardly ever venturing into the town. When the family did socialize, it was to go to church. "Even goin' to the movies was considered sinful," Dolly recalls. "But once a movie called *Thunder Road* was filmed right near us with Robert Mitchum. So daddy said we could see it when it was in town. I didn't enjoy the movie, though, because it seemed like I was breakin' a rule, and in a way so were mama and daddy."

A path snaked from Dolly's home to a spring where the family got their water. "We had a spring out back where we'd store the perishables, things like butter and milk. We didn't have no electricity either. And there was no yard—no backyard and no front yard. With twelve kids, how could grass grow? I remember always sayin' I'd like a nice yard. Mama would take a broom and sweep the yard. It's true! The yard was cleaned up when she'd take a broom and sweep it up, just like a floor.

"We also had a pumpkin patch, where we raised corn, beans, potatoes, and turnips. That was to eat. And we raised tobacco for money. And we canned a lot."

Once a year hogs were killed for food, but with fourteen mouths to feed in the Parton household, the meat did not last long.

"We never actually starved," recalls Dolly, "but

Globe Photos

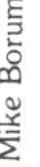

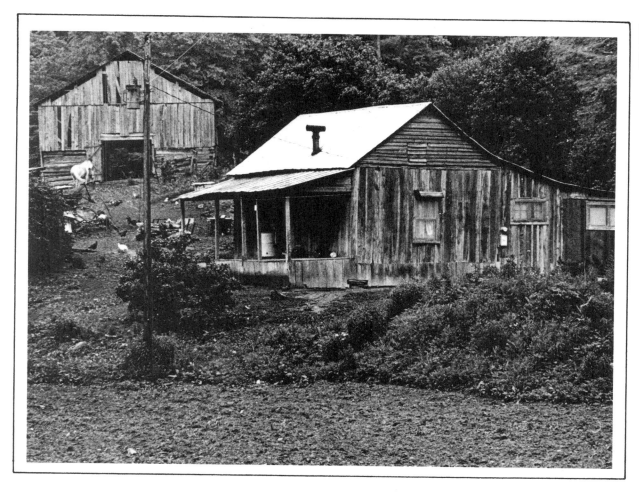

Dolly's home in Sevierville while she was growing up.

sometimes we never had quite enough to eat. . . . Never had much meat, mostly beans and potatoes, things like that. But we never went hungry, we were just hungry for a variety of things. But I still love things like biscuits and gravy."

But she emphasizes in that fetching Dolly Parton drawl, "We were *poor*. We had love and food to eat but otherwise, nothin'. A tube of lipstick would have been like a million dollars to me.

"Of course, because we were poor, there were unhappy moments. There were just plain hard times. Like when I'd see daddy work until his hands would bleed and bust open and he's down in the back. Or mama would be lyin' there sick with things that you can't afford a doctor to take care of. You can't see that sort of thing and have it not be painful for you and affect you.

"We didn't have nothin' material at all. We lived in shacks, moved from one to another. We even had a one-holer outhouse. If you were rich, then you had a two-holer. And we had no clothes, no real clothes. But we had a lot of each other and that's what counts.

"But life was good in its way at home. It was bad in its way, but also good. Naturally after you're grown and after you're successful you always tend to glorify a situation. And then the hard times don't seem to matter. It's the good that you remember, and the bad makes you a better person and makes you appreciate the good that comes later on. It's the balance of the good and the bad that makes you a person with depth and feelin' and also makes your life have meanin'. . . . And there was always love and security in my family. That was so important."

But the love and the security did not always compensate for the lack of material things and the often gritty earmarks of a poverty-stricken upbringing in the mountains. The memory of rats that scurried around in the bedroom at night, where Dolly and her brothers and sisters slept three and four to a bed, still persists. She sleeps with a night light on even today. And growing up in the backwoods, in moonshine country—Dolly's father made moonshine when he and her mother were first married—also brought with it some bucolic peculiarities. Dolly confesses there were some strange goings-on in the hollers where she lived and talks about knowing where there are "many shallow graves." As she once said, somewhat mysteriously, "I have seen things I wouldn't even tell in an interview. I have seen it all."

"Of course I suffered some like all poor people, by lack of material things, like the right kind of clothes and havin' to wear rags and hand-me-down things. But my parents were kind enough to try to make me feel good about it, no matter what. But there was no real solution to it at the time. Our attitude was the main thing. The fact that we cared and were cared for and knew to be humble. We knew, as they say, that if somebody smite you on one cheek, then you turn the other.

"There's always a certain amount of pain that goes along with anything, whether it be a job or growing up or whatever. The bad things just are pushed aside after a while, and they do give your life a meaning."

The scarcity of money in the Parton family was aggravated by Mama Parton's continual illnesses. Avie Lee Parton was sick so much of the time that Dolly was forced to assume the role of surrogate mother at an early age.

"Mama was sick a lot. She had so many kids, you know. I always say that mama was pregnant so much that she used to have one kid on her and one kid in her. And since she took sick, us older kids got to claim the next kid—that is, to take care of it within the family. Once mama got spinal meningitis and the doctor said there was no way she could live. But she did live. But the effects of it went to the baby she was carryin'. It was a little brother. When it was born it only lived nine hours. That really hurt me deep, 'cause I was at an age when I took things so hard. I was ten years old then, just tryin' to grow. . . . Daddy took it hard, too. It was the first time I saw him cry."

With their father working so hard and their mother spending so much time in a sick bed, the Parton children found themselves alone a lot. In many ways, Dolly was a lonely child—well not really lonely; she recalls that she never felt lonely, but she did while away many hours alone. To amuse herself, she made up stories and played out fantasies in her mind. She didn't have any books, but sometimes a relative or friend would bring by some magazines or newspapers and she would look at the pictures and use her fertile imagination to create lives for the people she saw. She remembers that she was entranced by anything shiny, golden, or fluttery— whether it was butterflies, cheap costume jewelry, hummingbirds, flowers, even the shiny quartz her father would find while plowing the field. They all captured her fancy. Since there was no television and no movies she could go to, she read fairy-tale books in school and the shimmering heroines in those storybooks became her ideals. When they got the battery radio working, the Partons would listen to "The Grand Ole Opry" or "The Lone Ranger" on radio. And Dolly would pore over a catalog and dream about the fancy things she would have when she was older and rich. "Mama called it the wishbook," she says, " 'cause it made you wish for things you didn't have.

"I used to love fairy stories, fairy tales," she recalls with a wistful sigh. "I used to just live in them. And I was so impressed by jewelry. Back then, I thought anyone who had a clean house was rich. Anything that glittered, glistened, I thought one day, I'd have that too. . . .

"Lookin' fancy was one way to fill up the days, and dreamin' was another. I kind of lived in a fairy tale. I was Cinderella or a princess. I wanted folks to

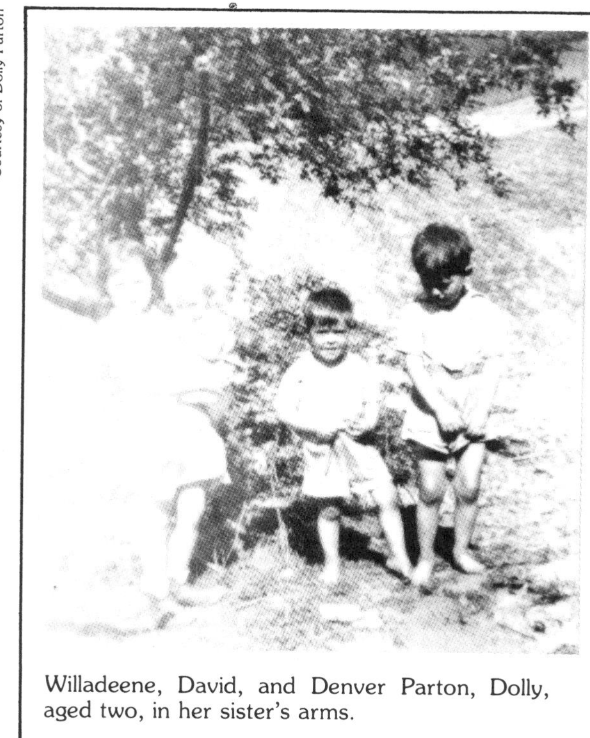

Courtesy of Dolly Parton

Willadeene, David, and Denver Parton, Dolly, aged two, in her sister's arms.

be happy to see me comin' and to remember me when I walked away. . . .

"I dreamed of the time that I'd have money and I'd be rich, and I would have pretty clothes and makeup and jewelry and cars and houses—big cars and houses. I just dreamed of all the things that I would have. And I dreamed of singin' and I dreamed of bein' famous and loved. It was like a fantasy life. I thought about bein' a king or a queen and just likin' people and havin' everybody like me.

"I was never a quiet-type person. I was never shy or backwards or bashful. I would talk to strangers and any kind of people. I also would sing anytime. I was more outgoin' than other kids, I think. But I did have my time for solitude. I would have my secret little places where I would go to write.

"I was just an independent type of kid, and that's the way I am now. I would get bored with all the clutter and the noise of kids hollerin' and screamin' and runnin' through the house, so I would often wander off by myself. I was afraid to go real far away so I just went to my secret places where I felt safe. I would go to write things or just to lie and look at the sky and watch the clouds floatin' by and I pretended they were all sorts of things. I liked to look real close at flowers and just enjoy the beauty of nature."

Probably Dolly also retreated to those private and "secret" places when something uncomfortable happened. Being poor often brought taunts from other children in the school, to which Dolly and her brothers and sisters walked a long way. Her grammar school had the first through the eighth grades all under one teacher—with about fifteen kids in the whole school. The grades went by rows, and the teacher would take turns teaching each row while the other children had to study.

"Sometimes you hated to go to school, because you were ashamed of the things you didn't have and kids would tease. But I'd make up a story to glorify the situation like I did with the song 'Coat of Many Colors.' " Dolly describes some of the childhood pain in songs like this and "The Good Old Days When Times Were Bad." She admits that no amount of money would be enough for her to go back and live through those times.

But the family life and the great love of her parents was there as a support, a means of carrying the Partons over the rough spots during their humble lives. Dolly glows with a real and deep daughterly love when she talks about her mother and her father.

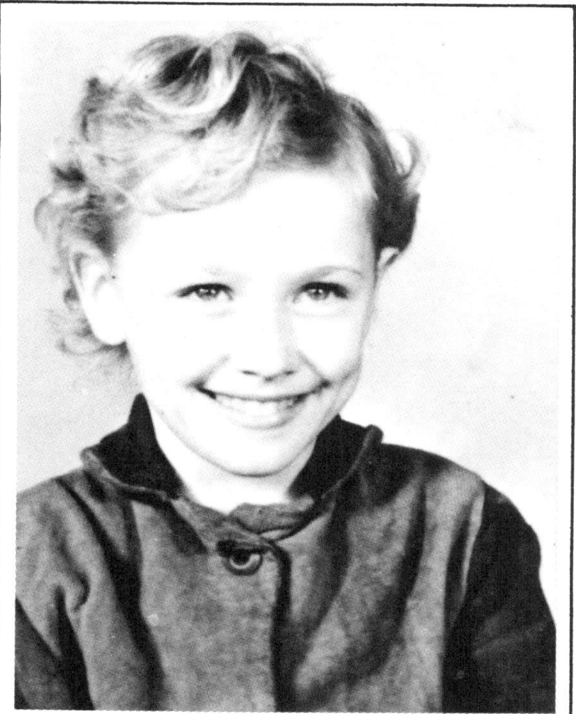

Courtesy of Dolly Parton

Dolly, aged eight, wearing the original coat of many colors.

"I think my mama and my daddy were the biggest influence in my life. They were just outstanding in my mind as a child. And they helped to mold and shape us as far as character goes. It was from them that we were all filled with love and life and energy and appreciatin' the things in nature. Just the least little thing we always seemed to appreciate. No matter it was so small that an average person would overlook it and take it for granted. We would know to notice all these things and I still do."

She describes her father as strict in his treatment of her. "He kept us in line. If we did somethin' bad, he whipped us with a belt. We'd have to go get the switch. But I was such, like I say, an independent kid, and I would do anything even if I knew I would get beat to death for it.

"My oldest sister Willadeene and myself were the oldest girls. And daddy didn't know how to be a daddy to teenage girls—especially because we were old-fashioned. He trusted us, but he just didn't trust other people. I guess he didn't want us to get prettied up and painted for fear that somebody would steal us away or somethin' like that. But then daddy got more mellow as time went on as daddies usually do, and he was less strict with the younger girls."

Dolly was early on fascinated with makeup and started wearing Merthiolate on her lips as make-believe lipstick. Real lipstick, anyway, would have been forbidden by her stern father. "It stung but it was worth the pain," she says. Her father would get mad and demand that she take if off, but she couldn't. And he couldn't rub it off either, so Dolly had her painted lips just like she wanted.

Despite these minor disagreements, Dolly portrays her father in rhapsodic terms. He was essentially plain, simple, and very much the country man; he could not read and write. With typical country superstition, he was wary of newfangled devices and wanted his children to be good and to behave. But he was country-shrewd as the mountain people can be. "He is the smartest man I ever knew," compliments his now-famous daughter. And he stood up to whatever hard times fate meted out to him and always took care of his wife and family.

"Thinkin' back on it I had a certain amount of fear of daddy," Dolly says. "If mama said 'I'm gonna tell your daddy when he gets home,' well, that would scare us and we'd spend the whole day tryin' to butter mama up so she wouldn't tell. Because we were afraid that Daddy would bust our ass. Now that I'm older, I think it's funny that I could have been afraid of daddy. It seems so strange to me."

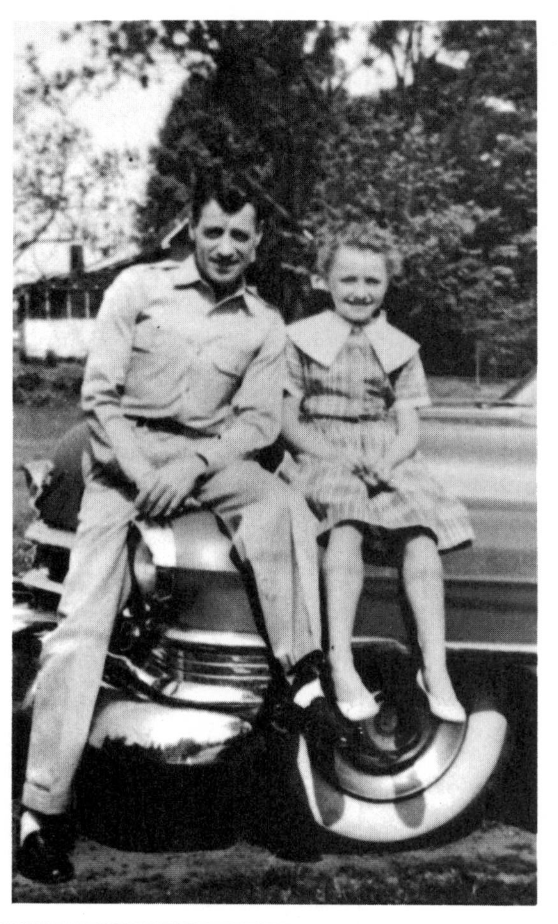

Mike Borum

Her mother, on the other hand, was more lenient. She was the daughter of a preacher and was used to the restrictions placed on children by straitlaced parents, so she understood how her children chafed at their father's strictness. She even fixed the clothes Dolly wore so that they would be tighter.

In a way, Dolly was much like her mother in that Avie Lee Parton was somewhat of a dreamer herself. She crooned Elizabethan ballads and believed in Dolly's ambition to become some kind of famous singing star. Dolly says she resembles her mother—she has her features, smile, and dimples—and she claims it is from her mother that she inherits her bouncy personality. But she also has her father's looks—it is his family that is fair with blue eyes and blond hair.

"Actually I think I'm a combination of mama and daddy in every way. And that combination also

Dolly's mother, Avie Lee Parton.

Dolly as a teenager with her father, "my favorite guy."

Courtesy of Dolly Parton

Mike Borum

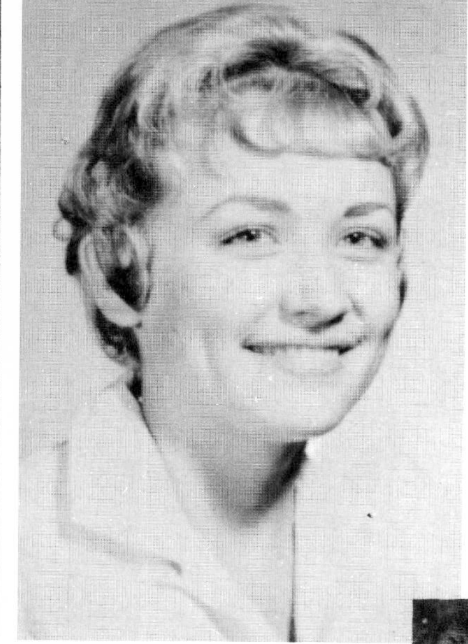

Dolly as a high school freshman (top left), sophomore (bottom left), junior (top right), senior (bottom right), and in her senior prom gown (center).

worked real well in our home—daddy was strict, but not too strict, and mama was lenient. I think it was a perfect balance. I'm glad that everything was the way it was. And the hard times just made all of us close like we are today. We are really all tied together."

Dolly recalls that she was not a particularly pretty child—not that she was really ugly, more that she was plain because of the lack of nice clothes. "I knew I could be pretty if I had the money and if I was rich. I think it's so with most country people who are poor. A lot of kids could have been beautiful, but they looked ugly because nobody knew how to take care of them. If you didn't have clothes to wear and you didn't have flattering hairstyles, you looked ugly. Or at least unattractive. In the summer your parents would whack off your hair, and there was no style or cut to it. That's the way it was with me. I guess thinkin' about it, I don't know if I was pretty or not 'cause how could I tell? But I don't remember dwellin' on whether I was pretty or ugly when I was a kid.

"I just think I could have been prettier if I had had clothes to wear then. I know I went through an ugly stage when I was about eight or nine, like every kid does. That's when your teeth are comin' in and they look like corn and you have to develop a bit."

Dolly did develop, and more than just a bit, when she was about twelve. Her chest blossomed in the bounteous way that has become one of her trademarks. "When I was thirteen, I looked like I was twenty-five," she says. "Really, I did." She remained five feet tall, although she remembers wishing that she could have grown taller, but she grew inches and inches on her bustline and her rump so that, entering adolescence, she had an almost exaggerated hourglass figure. That whistle-bait figure earned Dolly an undeserved reputation for being fast—people assumed that someone who looked like she did had to be up to a lot of naughty things.

"I had a lotta stories told on me, a lotta lies, just because I looked the way I did," Dolly confided to *Rolling Stone*. "I was always big in the boobs, small in the waist, and big in the butt. I just grew up that way and I had that foxy look."

She continues, "I got to lookin' real mature, and from then on I tried to improve my looks as much as I could and make the best of them. I wore my clothes skin tight—and I mean *skin tight*. I wore makeup and flirted a lot. Sometimes it was kind of embarrassin' to have the figure I did. But I knew that was just the way I was and had to accept it. Sometimes I thought people would be sayin' things behind my back. But it really didn't bother me all that much.

"I was popular in high school but not in the right way. I was the most popular girl in the county but not the kind of popular that wins class elections and gets voted things. Everybody was aware of me, though. It didn't bother me. I understood that I was misunderstood and also that I was really older than everybody else. Not only in looks but in attitude. I looked more mature and I was more mature. I was kind of serious, always writin' and dreamin' and plannin'.

"I also believed in sayin' and talkin' about things I believed in and speakin' my mind. If I wanted to tell a dirty joke, I did. Some parents thought I was a bad influence on their kids. But I was just older than my years and I related more to the teachers than the kids.

"I never really dated in high school. Maybe I had two dates all the time I was in school, and they were kids from school. Of course I did sneak off and had some boy friends on the side.

"I guess a lot of people thought I was mean and I wasn't. I was then just like I am now. I was open and honest and free. A lot of people can't stand that. Especially when you're that age. You can be a threat to people if you have a strong identity of your own. People want you to think just like them and be just like them and I wasn't. I just never went by anybody else's rules. Of course I would obey the rules, like I wouldn't smoke in the bathroom—I never smoked anyway—but I just wouldn't conform. I was different."

Dolly once said, "I never felt I belonged." But on speaking with her, it becomes obvious that the statement was not made out of any pain at being a nonconformist. She claims that being different did not upset her—it was just a fact. She accepted it, as she did her voluptuous figure. That was the way it was going to be and there was no changing it.

"I never fit in with cliques. Sometimes, you know, kids would run together, the most popular ones or the most intelligent ones or the ones who were good in sports. I was always an outsider. And I really didn't want to belong in other people's cliques. I just preferred to be myself and be an individual. If bein' an individual meant that I didn't get in their groups, well that was fine with me. I was just kind of a loner. I had some friends, but even my good friends I felt different from. They were usually just people I related to more than I did the others. It was because I was creative and independent and wanted to spend time on that; I didn't have time to worry about fittin' into anybody's groups."

Dolly was the first person in her family to be graduated from high school. She was never a scholar and didn't particularly care for school all that much, but she felt it was important to finish school "so I could say I did." She felt it would be useful before she set off into the world.

"I never failed anything. I could have been smart and got real good grades because I had the intelligence. But I was too involved with songwriting and stuff to study. I was probably about a C student. Certain things I would make better grades and certain things I would do worse. I got somethin' like a ninety-eight in band.

To make school a more pleasant experience, Dolly would play tricks and make up little jokes "just like I do today."

"I would disobey, not to upset anything, but to be mischievous. I was always real mischievous. I did little things for a joke.

"Like in home economics classes, I would be bored and I wanted to do something else. So I would cut up the fly swatter and paste it back together with staples so you couldn't see it. Then when the teacher would go to swat a fly, the swatter would go into pieces.

"Or one of the teachers would collect all the jaw breakers and chewing gum in class. You weren't allowed to have stuff like that, so he would take it up and put it on his desk. When I'd go by, I'd just pick them up, just take up some chewing gum and

Courtesy of Dolly Parton

Dolly in her sophomore year with her home economics classmates. Second from right, kneeling, is Judy Ogle who is now Dolly's secretary. Left: Dolly in her band uniform; she played the snare drums.

"I was just not involved enough and didn't study. I was bored by it. I wanted to get out."

Today Dolly confesses that the sight of a school bus is depressing to her, because it reminds her of all the kids cooped up in classrooms. And she admits that she would not like to have her own children go to school, even though she knows it would be necessary. But, as unhappy as she was in school, she says it was better than staying at home where her mother was ill so much of the time.

jaw breakers, and go sit down. I'd save 'em in my things for later. The teacher would often see me do it, but he didn't say anythin'. I think he would get a kick out of it. I was not a brat; I'd just do things a lot of times for the hell of it, or else I was tryin' to get away with things.

"I wasn't afraid, you know, and I respected my teachers. I just wanted to have a little fun. If I was called to the principal's office, I'd just go and I wouldn't be afraid. Everybody else would panic if they were called. But I didn't think anything could be so bad. I was never afraid of people because they were older than me or different or in some kind of high position. I was never afraid period."

While her interest in school dwindled, Dolly focused her tremendous energies on music. It was as much a flight from reality and yearning for beauty as watching the butterflies and wearing paint on her lips. Her father recalls, "She was singin' almost before she could talk." And her grandfather the preacher, the Reverend Jake Owens, echoes that reminiscence. "How long's Dolly been singin'? Why ever since she quit cryin'. That thing come here a singin'," he booms.

There was the musical tradition in the family. Her mother's family boasted a long line of singers, composers, and musicians. Some of her father's people played musical instruments, too. Her grandfather Owens taught music and was a prolific songwriter. Dolly has recorded some of his songs as has one of country's grandes dames, Kitty Wells.

"I've been in music all of my life. It's part of the family. My mama sings and my daddy and all of us kids, too."

Dolly maintains that she is not even the most talented one. She was just the first to think of making it a career and to become a success at it.

"I was just the one with the dreams and the confidence," she says. "From the time I was little I always loved music. And then I learned there was this place you could go to become a star. It was called Nashville. I always wanted to become a star. I always wanted a glamourous way of life. I wanted to be in the lights and the glitter and have beautiful clothes and jewelry and fat hairdos.

"Mama says that I was always singin' and that I was always makin' up songs. I was makin' up songs before I started for school, and mama would write them down for me. I always say I started writin' when I was five, but mama says I was makin' up songs after I learned to talk. The first song I wrote that I remember was called 'Little Tiny Tasseltop.' It was about a doll that mama had made for me out of a corn cob. I would make up songs about stories I heard, personal things I heard people say, about feelings and emotions.

"I just always had this gift of rhyme. And I was always thinkin' and noticin' what people were saying. I was always real curious."

Dolly translated the tragedies of country life into song—laments for a mother's son who had been killed in the war or a baby who had died of fever.

Courtesy of Dolly Parton

Dolly at the time of her arrival in Nashville, aged eighteen.

Her parents never scoffed at her dreams and her grandiose goals; and her mother was especially supportive.

"One fine thing about mama and daddy is they always let their children hold onto their dreams."

Dolly's vision of becoming a singing star was never dimmed by the thought that it might be difficult, especially for a rural hillbilly girl, to get ahead in show business. She was gutsy and fearless and determined. She just assumed she would be a success. As she once said, "I was afraid to be afraid of not makin' it."

When she was six, she fashioned her first guitar for herself. "I just took an old busted-up mandolin and a couple of guitar strings and I made me an instrument of some kind. I could get some sounds on it."

Her singing talents were further honed in church, the House of Prayer where her grandfather Jake Owens preached about "hell so hot you could feel the heat." Dolly joined the choir there when she was about six, although the word *choir* is a loose term for the impromptu and disparate crew that appeared for services with guitars in tow. They strummed and sang away regular hymns and religious songs of their own creation.

This country, fundamentalist brand of religion was a significant force in shaping Dolly's character and her music. The almost evangelical aspect of her I-can-do-anything-I-set-my-mind-to attitude reflects a kind of deep, inner faith. She often displays a celestial optimism even in her most secular songs; there's an exhortative quality that seeps through in the tunes about grittier and grimmer topics. She talks a lot about evil and goodness, concepts that were instilled in her youthful church-going.

Courtesy of Dolly Parton

Dolly during her plain stage.

Dolly has often credited her boisterous preacher grandfather with influencing her music. "I always loved and respected him," Dolly says. "He was such a joyful person. He was very involved with music and had a great personality. He would love to write and sing and I related to him a great deal."

The creed of her grandfather's church was not shaped by any particular body of thought but was instead dictated by reading the Bible. Dolly liked to read the stories in the Bible; and often she and her brothers and sisters would pretend they were disciples or characters in the Old Testament. The Bible was just another marvelous storybook that inspired Dolly's imagination.

As she described her family religion, to the *Village Voice*, "It was a Church of God assembly but we never held to no doctrine really, except by scripture. You have to go by scripture. We just believed to make a joyful noise unto the Lord and that's what we did.

"Our services would be mostly music, different families, different individuals gettin' up to sing. The old hymns. Above that they was just about the biggest thing we did recreation-wise. The house I lived in when I was little we had to walk four miles to the mailbox. So church was a social event. More than just Sunday; we'd have revivals, prayer meetings services different evenings of the week."

Today Dolly states emphatically, "Of course I believe in God. And if I've got soul at all, it's country soul and it comes from church."

When she was singing at church and refining her performing skills in the spiritual arena, she'd trill for an invisible audience. Her mother once recalled that Dolly would sit perched high on a tree limb as a youngster and sing away in that curious high-pitched soprano. The make-believe concerts made her dreams seem more of a reality. "I had an ambition and it burned inside me," she recalls. Part of her youthful rambunctiousness, part of her capriciousness, was due to that itching desire to get out of her small town and make her way into the world. But she had to be ready.

Even before she was in high school, Dolly started working on her ambition. When she was ten, her uncle Bill Owens took her to Knoxville where she auditioned for one of the local radio shows. "They liked me a lot; I knew they would. I started workin' that radio show mostly in the summertime, and I could stay with my aunt and uncle. They paid me about twenty dollars a week. I used to stand up and sing all by myself — songs I wrote myself, and other country songs. I played the guitar. When I was about eleven, I guess, I made my first record. It was called 'Puppy Love.' Then when I was in high school I made another record for Mercury Records and it was called — get ready — 'It May Not Kill Me but It's Sure Gonna Hurt.' My Uncle Bill was responsible for both of those records."

It was also her Uncle Bill who borrowed a car and drove Dolly to Nashville one day so that she could sing at the Grand Ole Opry.

"I remember I was wearin' a blue silk dress. I went backstage with my guitar and Uncle Bill told people there that I wanted to sing. Everybody said

Dolly with her grandfather, the Reverend Jake Owens, who was the inspiration for the song, "Daddy Was an Old Time Preacher Man."

that I couldn't do that, that there was no way I could get out on stage and sing. They said I wasn't in the union. Finally I talked to a singer named Jimmie C. Newman and he was goin' to sing next. He let me have one of his spots. I sang 'If You Want to Be My Baby' and the audience clapped and clapped. I guess I was kinda scared, but I kept thinkin' about mama and daddy and my brothers and sisters back home, all of them listenin' to me on the radio and that made me excited. I really felt like I was a star and here I was on the 'Grand Ole Opry' and everything."

That appearance on the "Grand Ole Opry" helped Dolly nourish her dreams of stardom. It was a farfetched goal for a simple country girl like herself, especially since people in the mountains never thought of breaking away from their quiet and plain lives. It was just beyond their ken. When Dolly told people with her flinty determination that she was going to become a star, she recalls that they replied, "Well, it's nice to daydream, but don't get carried away." But Dolly did allow herself to be carried away, buoyed along by sheer force of her own weighty self-confidence and her experience at the radio show in Knoxville. She sang there until she was eighteen, at station WIVK, on a program called "The Farm and Home Hour," for a man named Cas Walker who owned a chain of supermarkets.

Courtesy of Dolly Parton

Dolly on her high school graduation night.

At various times during her high school years, Dolly's uncle drove her to Nashville and she trudged up and down the streets, trying to get people to listen to her sing. Sometimes she and Uncle Bill would have to sleep in the car overnight, since they had no money for a hotel room. The next morning she would freshen up and wash and put on makeup in the ladies' room of a gas station. Then the rounds would begin once more, up and down Music Row, as the cluster of producers' and record company offices are called, with Dolly led by her uncle. After the rounds were made, she would invariably go to look at the names on the pavement around the Country Music Hall of Fame. In her head she vowed that someday her name would be there, along with other country music giants like Kitty Wells and Johnny Cash.

Dolly could have quit school and gone to Nashville right away. But something held her back. Despite the fact that she hated book learning and was terribly bored in school, she just felt that it would be good to finish and at least know what a high school graduate was supposed to know.

On the night of Dolly's high school graduation in June 1964, each member of the departing senior class was invited to announce their plans for career

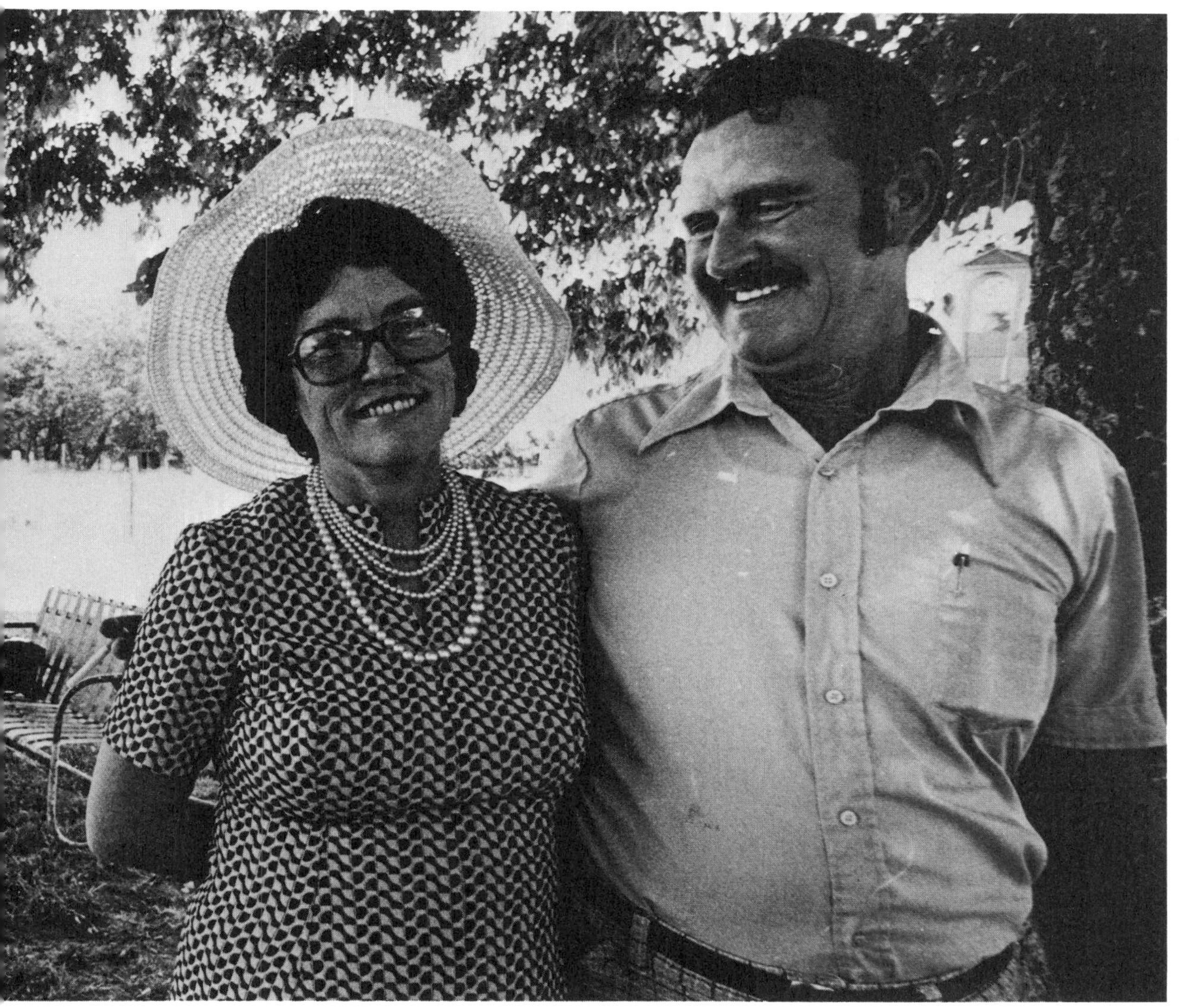

Globe Photos

Dolly's parents, Robert and Avie Lee Parton, in a recent picture taken on their farm thirty miles outside Nashville.

and postgraduation life. Most talked about getting married or modest hopes for simple jobs. But Dolly declared her matter-of-fact view of her coming success — she was going to Nashville to become a star in country music. Her sister Willadeene remembers that people started snickering and laughing when Dolly said that. Why, they wondered, was this snare drummer in the Sevier County High band and a member of the Future Homemakers of America, dreaming that she could go into show business?

But the laughs did not daunt Dolly one bit. "I just knew I could make it," she says. "I had a whole lot of confidence, no matter what nobody said, and I believed I could do it. And if you don't think you can do something, nobody else will."

Right after Dolly made her serious pronouncement about entering show business in front of an audience of skeptics, she went home to pack a few belongings and her songs in a cardboard suitcase fastened with string. That was on Friday. Early the next Saturday morning Dolly was on the bus to Nashville, some two hundred miles away. She never turned back.

Nashville Beginnings

In Nashville, Dolly Parton of the mountains was to meet the two men who would probably become the most important and influential in her life — country music star Porter Wagoner and a young, hustling businessman named Carl Dean. The two men could not have been more different—Porter was a slick, rhinestone-studded cowboy crooner, and Carl was a modest, quiet type, utterly removed from the show business way of life. The meeting with Carl came just a few hours after she arrived in Nashville, an eager hopeful from Sevierville with cardboard suitcase in-hand. The fortuitous encounter with Porter Wagoner came about three years after her debarkation in the country-music mecca.

As soon as Dolly stepped off the Greyhound bus, she headed for the area called South Nashville, where her uncle Bill have moved with his wife and young child just several weeks earlier. Bill Owens, who had sung professionally at county fairs and club events with his two brothers Louis and Robert, had his own small band. He traveled around the counties playing his guitar and singing, and writing songs in his spare time. He was the one who had really encouraged Dolly, shepherding her to Nashville as a youngster, teaching her chords on the guitar, helping her get appearances on radio shows, working on songs with her occasionally.

Today, Dolly, always one to credit those who have aided her in her career, says, "Everything, or at least a lot of things, that I did in the early part of my career, he was responsible for. Of course it might have happened anyway, but there's a chance it might not have happened if it hadn't been for him."

But Bill Owens wasn't there to greet Dolly that first day in Nashville, nor was his wife. Bill was out traveling with his band, and Dolly's aunt had a job at the local Shoney's restaurant. In return for food and shelter, Dolly was to babysit for their little boy.

After settling down in her uncle's apartment, Dolly set out to find a laundromat. She had such a small wardrobe at the time that most of the clothes she'd brought from Sevierville were not only well worn but dirty. And besides, she was in a rush to get to Nashville so she didn't have time to pack properly — she'd just crammed all her clothes, clean or not, into the suitcase along with her songs. So, that first day in Nashville, Dolly was off to the Wishy-Washy. After she got her clothes into the machine, she decided to explore her new home.

"I was walkin' down the street, lookin' at everything. I didn't know what city life was going to

Mike Borum

Dolly with Porter Wagoner.

be like, and that was exciting to me. Anyhow, I saw this handsome man drive by in a white car. So I waved to him, because I'm by nature a friendly person. When you're from the country, like I am, you just wave to people and say 'hi.' It's not flirtin', it's just bein' friendly. You just would talk to everybody who goes by.

"This guy waved back and then hollered at me. And then he came over to talk to me."

But Dolly, bearing the old-fashioned strictures of her father in mind, did not rush into things. "I couldn't go out with him, because it wouldn't have been right. I said to him, 'I can't go out with you; I don't even know you.' You just did not do things like that if you were from the country. You had to be careful. But I told him that he could come over to Uncle Bill's house and sit with me while I was babysittin' my nephew. That was just the way I knew to do things.

"I loved Carl the first time I saw him. It was one of those old stories — love at first sight. He felt the same way about me. He told me that the minute he saw me he knew that I was the one for him.

"He was just somebody that totally impressed me. Of course, I liked the way he looked. I've always liked real slender men, and Carl is like that. He's skinny as a rail and tall. He's kind of the opposite of me, but I've heard that's the way it is, that you're attracted to the opposite of yourself. And I liked his personality right from the start. There's some people who are drawn to each other immediately and that's the way it was with us and it's been that way ever since.

"Anyway, every day that week, he would come up to the house in the afternoons. We would sit outside on the porch and talk. I didn't go in the house with him because that wouldn't have been right. I knew not to do things like that. When my aunt got a day off, Carl and I went out on a real date. At least it was the first time we'd ever been out together. He took me to his parents' house, and I was introduced to them. We knew we were just so right for each other. I guess you could say he was my first real boy friend."

But as deeply as she felt for Carl, she was uncertain about marriage. She knew what she wanted — a career in show business — and that did not allow for a conventional marriage where the wife was home all the time and raised a large family. She realized that she would be traveling on the road as a country singer and felt it would not be right to have a husband under those circumstances. And she was unsure that her career allowed for her to have children—ever.

"I did love him, but I didn't think it would be fair to marry him," she said. But then she added with typical country philosophy, "But you know how love goes." Carl insisted that Dolly's way of life didn't matter and assured her that he would never expect her to change her ways or conform to typical marriage standards or give up her career. He told her he just wanted to be with her. About two years later, after Carl had finished a stint in the army, Dolly Parton became Mrs. Carl Dean.

Things did not happen quite so quickly for Dolly professionally. She came to Nashville with her typical irrepressible confidence and optimism, but she did not become an overnight success.

"The first few months I was afraid, but my determination was greater than my fear, and my confidence was greater than my fear. I knew I would have a hard time, but when you're used to doin' without, you don't get afraid of what you're gonna have to do without. I was uncertain about the city life. But I was lucky; I had all the confidence in the world that I would make it.

"But those were not easy times. I used to walk up and down the streets of Nashville, knockin' on doors, tryin' to get people to listen to my songs. When people wouldn't listen to them, I'd just say to myself, 'They don't know yet but they will.' I guess they thought I was too country to be country."

Sometimes, even with her positive attitude, Dolly became discouraged. She recalls the time she lived for about two weeks on mustard and horse relish and other foods "you have in the refrigerator to eat alongside with somethin' else." Sometimes she thought she'd starve to death. And then there were nights she would cry herself to sleep, tired, frustrated, and lonely. She would write letters home suffused with the ache of her homesickness. One of them, featured on her album *Tennessee Mountain Home*, reads, "I'm fine, I guess, just a little lonesome and a whole lot homesick. I didn't realize how hard it was to leave home till I started to leave and everybody started crying, including me."

But Dolly, through her talent and her incredible persistence, progressed. "About six months after I got to Nashville, I did get on salary with a publishing company. That was with Fred Foster, who owned Monument Records and Combine Publishing Company. That was for about fifty dollars a week; it was enough to make it, but not much else. And

Mike Borum

then I started singin' on a local television show in Nashville called 'The Eddy Hill Show.' And things just started pickin' up."

Foster was doing well producing the records of a guitar-playing singer named Roy Orbison, who earned an estimable reputation among both country and rock fans for songs like "Pretty Woman" and "Runnin' Scared."

The Dolly Parton whom Fred Foster hired then was a far cry from the self-assured and dazzling professional performer that is so popular today.

"She was very shy and inexperienced when she came to Monument—she didn't know much of anything about stage presence or makeup or things like that—but I thought she was the freshest, most distinctive thing I'd seen. I don't think she had any idea what her potential was, but she did at least realize that she was a little bit different, that she didn't sound like anybody else. And she saw no reason why she couldn't become a star," Foster once recalled.

Finally, in pursuit of singing and writing and recording, Dolly achieved a modest hit called "Dumb Blonde." It probably echoed Dolly's own feelings as a neophyte in Nashville, with the city folk deeming her somewhat of a country hick. "I was so

country myself I didn't fit in," she recalls. "I knew they thought I was dumb. They laughed at the way I talked. But it didn't matter, 'cause I knew how smart I was."

"Dumb Blonde" was written by a composer named Curly Putnam. It was a novelty tune and had lyrics that urged people not to think this blond was dumb because she was blond, " 'cause this dumb blond ain't nobody's fool."

"Dumb Blonde" was the first of Dolly's records to make the country charts. She quickly followed it up with a sassy little number called "Something Fishy," which landed in the country top twenty. In that song, the singer accuses her guy of hanky-panky during fishing trips. Although it did not display Dolly's most sensitive songwriting ability, "Something Fishy," her first own composition to make a dent among the public, was cute and enjoyable. When she recorded it in the Monument studios, some of Nashville's most accomplished and respected songwriters were there to listen. Dolly was beginning to get attention in Nashville.

Perhaps it was the minor success of songs like these that caught the attention of Porter Wagoner, who gave Dolly what she acknowledges as "my first real big break."

Porter selected Dolly to replace a perky blond girl singing partner named Norma Jean, who was leaving Porter's popular syndicated television show to get married and move to Oklahoma. The position promised Dolly invaluable exposure since Porter's show was a popular staple among country fans. Dolly had heard about his television program back in Sevierville and recalled that as a youngster he was someone the neighbors regarded as a really big star.

Porter also got RCA to pick up her contract from Monument Records at the sum of a mere hundred dollars a week. But even that meager amount was hard for Porter to secure. Chet Atkins, the guitarist who had become one of the executives at RCA, told Porter flatly "I don't think the girl can sing." Atkins was unimpressed by Dolly's tapes. But Porter insisted on Dolly's being signed by RCA, even going so far as to insure RCA against incurring any losses. He told Atkins that if RCA lost any money at all on Dolly, they could take it out of Porter's royalties. "I know the girl can sing," he declared to Atkins.

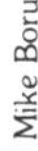
Mike Borum

Porter and Dolly was a felicitous pairing, not only of singers but also of images—Porter with that rich, slick pompadour and tapestries of country life studded in rhinestone on his denim outfits, lanky and swaggering with country bravado, slim as a tumbleweed. And then Dolly, petite with that remarkable bosom and curvaceous frame, a little doll-like lady dressed in fancy country-style gowns, the kind of clothes she'd longed for as a kid. And her presence was always surmounted by that towering mountain of golden hair, sculpted and curled high. They complemented each other so perfectly and worked together in such harmonious teamship that many people thought Porter and Dolly were man and wife off the show. She was Porter's sidekick for about seven years, and during that time Dolly probably logged up more hours with him than she did with her own husband. Inevitably there were rumors about a romance between them, and the rumors were exacerbated by the fact that he bought her diamond rings. And she wore them proudly, on all of her fingers, except the one that had the wedding ring from Carl.

At first Dolly was upset about the gossip, the talk that she and Porter were lovers. "It did bother me for a while, but then it just got to be old stuff, like everything else," she admits. "Of course, I wasn't used to people talkin' about me like that. But I figured the people who knew me would know the difference, and people who didn't know me, well, if they said anything, it wouldn't matter anyway. My husband always knew what the truth was. I figure that if there had been anything between me and Porter, my husband would have been the first to know it, because you cannot deceive people."

What Dolly did share with Porter was an abiding love of music and a drive for fame and success. As she once said, "People have always thought there was somethin' goin' on with me and Porter. There was a great love between me and Porter, but it was not the kind of situation that people always thought it was. It was unique. It was a unique respect and love and involvement with each other. Because we were so much the same kind of person."

And she revealed with typical Dolly Parton honesty, "I'm not ashamed to say that I care for Porter, but it is definitely not the kind of carin' that I went to bed with him. He's the kind of person that I could lay across the bed with him and sleep forever and not ever touch him in the kind of way that people always think that male and female do. That you have to be able to have sex in order to have a relationship—that is not true."

What is true is that through Porter's show and her association with him, Dolly began to achieve an important level of fame and recognition as a country performer. They had a playful relationship on the air that captivated the audience—Porter was respectful but obviously appreciative of Dolly's full-blown femininity and would call her Miss Dolly. For her part, Dolly projected a shy innocence, especially during those first years of the partnership, when she would dress in frilly crinolines and gathered skirts drawn tight at the waist. He would gallantly offer to hold Dolly's guitar while she sang an a-cappella solo; she would reply, the essence of demureness, "No indeed, that's my security blanket."

There were lighthearted moments of humor as well, as when once a dancing fiddler appeared on the show and his bow got stuck in one of those gigantic waves of her hair.

Porter had never sung any duets with Norma Jean, but now with Dolly they sang together all the time. And to his credit, he did not hesitate to break down barriers for Dolly so that she could realize as much success as possible. He scoffed at those listeners who failed to appreciate the shimmery vibrato that was her unique vocal quality.

As he once described Dolly's talent, "Dolly's is a hard voice to capture on record—very piercing, gives the equipment a fit. It's Dolly's register. I can't hardly place Dolly in any vocal tradition. She's very unique."

And he obviously felt that their singing could not have been better. As he rhapsodized, "Our harmony is so close it's almost blood kin. Brother and sister, you know, harmonize better than a great tenor and a great lead singer gettin' together. . . . Dolly and her sisters, for instance, can sing closer harmony than any professional singers in Nashville. Dolly and I sound nearly like brother and sister."

The relationship between Porter and Dolly was more give-and-take than a first superficial evaluation would reveal. It was not simply a matter of mentor and protegée, but more a matter of helping each other in various areas. Each benefited from the other's talents—Dolly from Porter's fame and well-established reputation and his knowledge of working an audience. And Porter gained from her songwriting ability and the fact that as Dolly became more of a personality, she enhanced his appeal. Dolly so inspired Wagoner that he was propelled to begin composing again after a hiatus of almost twenty years.

While acknowledging Porter's vast influence and his assistance, Dolly today maintains, "Porter helped me to become a star, but I don't feel he made me a star."

She continues, "I think I learned a lot of things from Porter. He was good to me in many ways. I always give him the credit for givin' me a big break. I don't know if it's the right way of sayin' it, but he was also bad for me in many ways, though. We had our hard times. He was a stubborn person set in his ways, like I am in mine. We were actually alike in many ways."

"At the time he hired me, he didn't actually know I was a songwriter. So he was helped in that area from me. As time went on, I became a publisher and I gave him half of that publishing company, called Owepar, a combination of my daddy's and my mama's last names.

"He worked hard on my career because he believed in what I could do and I believed in him,

Dolly in an appearance on "The Porter Wagoner Show."

too. I tried to help him in ways I could and tried to write songs that would be good for both him and me. I provided songs for us to do as duets. It wasn't as if he was doin' me a favor by recording my songs. Nobody with any sense would record a song if it's not good enough. And Porter has lots of sense, and lots of ambition, too. So I had all these songs which Porter was not even aware of when I first started with him.

"But I learned a lot from him. I learned a lot about stage presence, and I learned a lot about the ins and outs of the business. He inspired me. I will always admire and respect him for those reasons and just because I will always love him in my own way.

"But there were certain qualities I didn't like about Porter. Just like I'm sure there were certain qualities about me that he didn't like. We got to arguin' and quarrelin' a lot towards the end. We just didn't get along so well then. He pulled things that were part of me to the surface, tempers and things like that. Things I never realized were a part of me. But how can you regret somethin' like that? A person that will drag all your emotions to the surface has got to be good for you in the end. It's enough to make you want to kill him when it's happenin', but then you go back over it and you realize how much you did grow and things like that. I wanted to do things the way I wanted, and he wanted to do things his way, and it was as much my fault as it was his fault."

In 1974 Dolly left Porter's group and his show in a move that was as shocking to country fans as the breakup of the Beatles was to rock fans. She wanted to do things on her own, and she also wanted to make more money. Although Dolly was making, according to her reckoning, about $300 a night when she worked for Porter and thus some $60,000 a year, she felt she could make more. It was a huge sum of money to a country girl who had grown up with no money, but that intrinsic self-confidence made her know that she shouldn't settle for hundreds and thousands when she could make hundreds of thousands.

The country-music business is as rife with rumors and gossip as any other area of the entertainment industry—and all sorts of controversy and tales surrounded the events behind Dolly's leavetaking. There were stories of a vicious lovers' quarrel and reports that bitter disagreements led to the split. Porter, it was said, was violently opposed to her going solo.

Dolly confirms this when she says, "Porter knew

UPI

From left: Roy Clark, Merle Haggard, Dolly, and Porter at the CMA Annual Awards in Nashville, 1970.

I was leavin', and he didn't like it. I had tried to work things out with him, and he just wouldn't listen. We'd just been fightin' for a few years, and we were both so stubborn. Finally, because he wouldn't talk to me, I just decided that I was just gonna go the best way I knew how. And then I'd be a personality like he was and still is. I just went ahead and did it 'cause I knew he was never gonna give me permission to do it.

"So then when I left he made a bigger thing than it was. I did try to work it out with him, and I did not do him wrong in any way. No more wrong than he did me. So I sort of feel it's all even. He did a lot of things for me and he did a lot of things to me, and I'm sure it was the same with him."

Porter, it seems, may be feeling hurt and bitter about the towering success of the greenhorn singer he first introduced to national audiences back in 1967 on his show. Clearly, he's ambivalent about the fact that Dolly Parton's name is a much bigger one today than that of Porter Wagoner.

As he confessed recently to *Country Style* magazine, "I'd be less than truthful if I said I wasn't disappointed in the way the relationship turned out. I put a lot of energy into making her records great and my own records suffered. . . . I don't expect anything from her. But someone you've worked with that long, you'd like for them to say hello to you," revealing that he hadn't seen Dolly in quite some time.

Dolly agrees that things today are not what they once were between her and Porter. "We're not as friendly as I would like to be. We're not enemies or anything like that, but we just don't see each other. Porter's real stubborn, and he never did forgive me for leavin'. I've seen a few articles in magazines where he kind of condemned me and said things that just were not true. He just told his side of it. Like he said I didn't say good-bye, or that I never said hello. Neither one was true.

"Porter still owns half of the publishing company, and he has a percentage of record royalties, so there's no way anybody could say that I cheated him. If anybody knew the actual story, nobody would say things like that. All the business things would be true to my story. But Porter's pride just wouldn't let him accept this.

"We could have worked it out," says Dolly, a shade wistfully about the man she was once so close to, "if he had worked at it and had been willin'. I was certainly willin'. But he couldn't, so things are like they are."

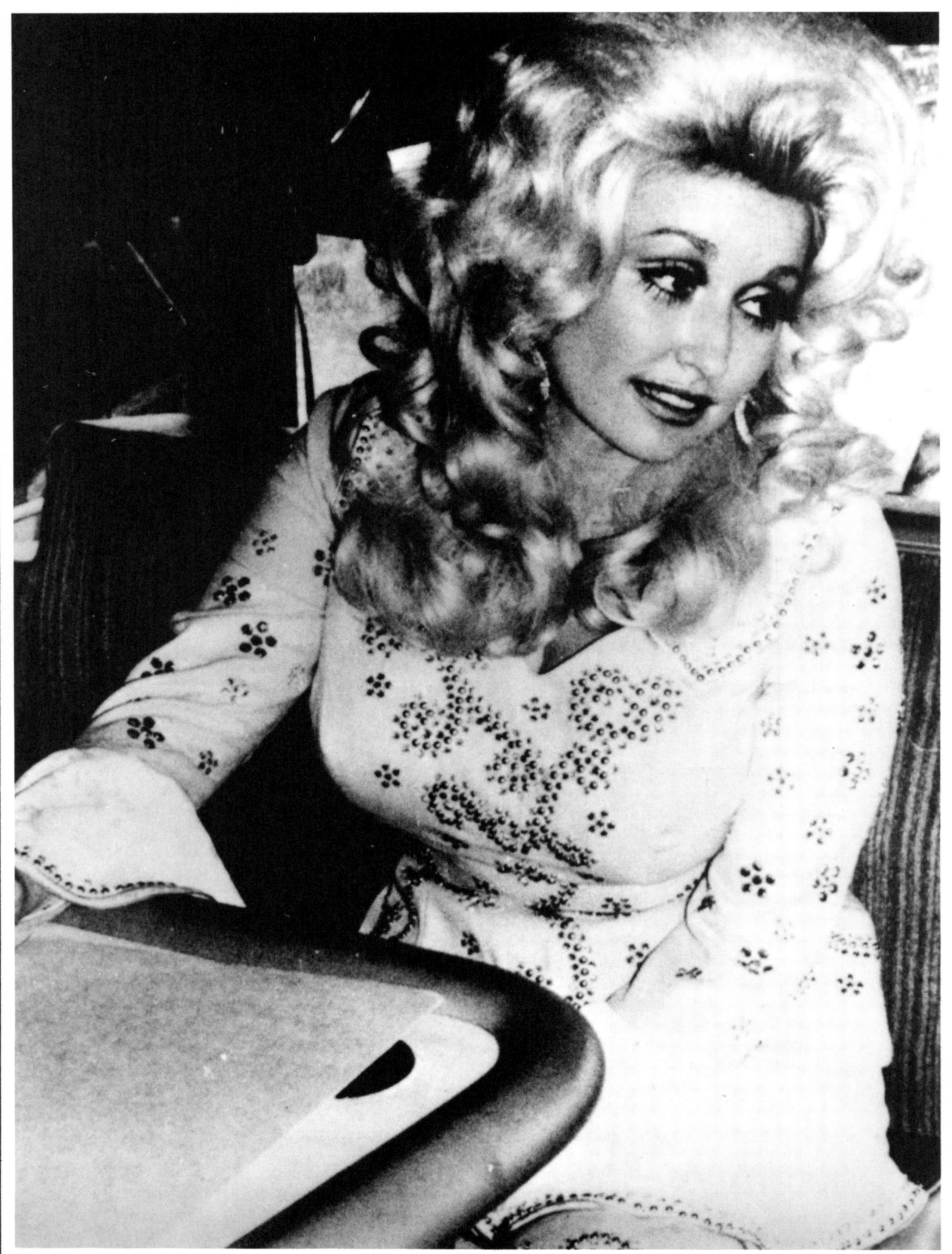

Making It Big

In 1974 Dolly Parton began to establish herself as a prominent separate entity in the country-music world, away from the figure of Porter Wagoner. More importantly, 1974 was the year that Dolly started to work toward her goal of national celebrity in more than just the country arena, as an entertainer appreciated from fans of pop to fans of rock. She began achieving status as a personality with an ever-growing cult of admirers.

The year 1974 was also when Dolly recorded her biggest hit, "Jolene," a ballad about a woman who tried to steal her man. It was a sad yet feisty song, with a bit of Dolly's own spiritedness in the face of no matter what, and it became the number-one country song of 1974.

In autumn of 1974 Dolly made the journey from Nashville to New York for a concert at the Felt Forum. Her popularity at that point was growing but hardly massive—she didn't fill the hall. But just a year later Dolly had garnered a stunning array of music awards that certified her success as an important country singer. She was named the Country Music Association's Female Vocalist of the Year. The trade papers of the music world, *Billboard, Cash Box,* and *Record World,* all named her top country vocalist of 1975. In addition, *Billboard* had cited her as Best Female Singles Artist and Best Songwriter in the Female Category.

At that point, her music was still very much in the country mold. She had not yet attempted to cross over into the pop world. In fact, in 1975, she was active in ACE—the Association of Country Entertainers—where she protested Olivia Newton-John's winning of a country award. Then an unadulterated country singer, Dolly maintained that Olivia wasn't a true country singer. Today Olivia, who has also recorded "Jolene," and Dolly are close friends.

Dolly has emerged as the fastest-rising star in country. Along with other Nashville empresses like Loretta Lynn and Tammy Wynette, Dolly assumed a position as one of country's queens. Loretta Lynn was dubbed "the coal miner's daughter," and Dolly became the favorite from the Smoky Mountains.

In addition to the homage paid her singing talents, Dolly's vast songwriting abilities began to be recognized. Although strongly autobiographical, her songs were recorded by a variety of artists, from the country to pop to rock fields—among them Maria Muldaur, Emmylou Harris, Linda Ronstadt, and Olivia Newton-John.

To go out on her own, Dolly had assembled a group to accompany her called the Travelin' Family

Band. The name was appropriate since the group included four siblings, an uncle, and a cousin. Dolly and her familial entourage took to the road for cross-country concerts that would bring the talents of the inimitable Miss Parton to all manner of public.

The appeal of Dolly Parton was rapidly growing—so much so that she was approached by Bill Graham, whose company Show Biz Inc. was responsible for producing Porter Wagoner's television show. With Graham's help and resources, Dolly launched her own syndicated country music TV show in 1976. The show was picked up by no less than sixty-four city stations, including such Yankee bastions as Detroit and New York. Called simply "Dolly!," it was the highest budgeted syndicated show ever produced in Nashville, costing some $85,000 to $100,000 per half hour. The show increased Dolly's popularity and better established her image—what she likes to say is her "outrageous" personality.

Dolly came off as a bounteous country soul, a happy, perky, delightful hostess, who bubbled over with an enthusiasm that was infectious. She was also revealed as a strong-minded woman who may have dressed oddly or somewhat bizarrely but was all the more interesting because of that trait. Graham said Dolly always had an uncanny knack for putting even the most nervous of her guests at ease and said that her giggly yet sunny aura easily made her the most popular personality in Nashville.

Success came in abundance, but it was not easily earned. She would put in some eighteen-hour days and was traveling on her bus, as do the majority of country performers, about forty weeks out of the year. She logged hundreds of thousands of miles and some weeks would wake up every day in a different town. "I guess I am a workaholic," she would say but then speak of her desire to make her music heard and become a vital force in the entertainment industry.

"Someday I'll retire," she vows. When? "Oh, in about eighty years," she laughs jauntily, "when I have done all that I want to do. But that keeps changin' and growin' all the time."

One thing that did not change was Dolly's appearance, which, if anything, grew more extreme with the passing of time. Some observers assumed that Dolly would tone down her mode of dress once she was somewhat established in the music field, but as she became more popular she felt freer to express herself as bizarrely as she wanted, to be as different as she could imagine.

"There's a reason for the way I dress," she says. "And I don't want to change. I could just see myself gettin' gaudier and more bizarre as time goes by. I like to be gaudy; it makes me different. When I first started singin' I decided I would dress in gaudy, outrageous clothes because that fit my outgoing personality. It was also like a dream come true. I always wanted to be glittery and stand out. Why should I hide the parts of me that are extreme? I just try to make the more extreme more extreme. Life, you know, can be kinda borin', so I like to spice up things.

"It's a gimmick, but if nobody can see what's there beyond the wigs and makeup, they're not very much of a person anyway. People who know me and like me know it's all a bunch of baloney. And now I'll do anything I want to do. If I want to wear lots of wigs and lots of makeup and just any kind of thing like that. Just be really darin' and adventurous."

In 1977 Dolly made her most daring move of all. She broke with her old band and hired a new one and announced that she was going to make an attempt to cross over. Dolly Parton of the Smoky Mountains was planning to go after fans in the pop spectrum and the rock spectrum.

Immediately the criticism flared up, especially among country purists who regard anyone who tries to gather a following among the pop field as a damnable defector. Dolly was accused of "going Hollywood" and turning her back on the fans who had always loved and supported her and the country folk who had helped her to grow. But country-music fans can be suspicious and narrow-minded people. Some of them consider any attempt to bridge the gap between country and pop as a slap in the face. They accuse performers who do so of tainting their music. It was not an easy decision for Dolly to make in the first place, and the salvos of criticism made the aftermath even more painful.

"I was just dreamin' big dreams," she says. "The decisions were hurtful to make. The changes I made weren't against the people I was with, but I just had to make these changes. It was hard for me to do it, and I suffered, but the suffering has been worthwhile. I don't like to hurt nobody's feelings, and I have a great love for all the people involved. But now I feel like an eagle who's trying to fly as high as it can."

Dolly performs with Roy Clark on the CMA show in 1976.

Dolly receives a gold disc for "Just Because I'm a Woman" in 1971, while doing a show for the Dolly Parton Scholarship Foundation in Sevier County.

Right: Dolly on the CMA show in 1977.

Courtesy of Dolly Parton

The upheaval began in 1976 when nodes on Dolly's vocal chords flared up and her doctors advised either a long period of rest or else surgery. Surgery on nodes is an extremely risky undertaking since it can irrevocably alter the timbre and style of a singer's voice. Certainly, Dolly's unique shimmery soprano is a voice quality to be treasured, so she opted for the rest cure. She canceled some sixty-five bookings for the period between mid-June and October. She was so careful to abide by her doctor's rules that she barely spoke during that period, communicating by notepad instead.

Yet, while Dolly was silent most of the time, her mental wheels were rapidly turning. It was evident that she was giving a great deal of thought to planning her career. Now that she was thirty, she figured some changes had to be made. The network of Nashville observers rippled with speculation about what these changes were to be. When the announcement was finally made in early 1977, criticism of Dolly Parton was at times unfairly harsh and bitter.

She had replaced her Travelin' Family Band with a new and more professionally seasoned group of Nashville musicians called Gypsy Fever. She had broken with her old Nashville managers and hired the prestigious Hollywood management firm of Katz, Gallin, and Cleary, who handle such impressive show business luminaries as Cher, and Mac Davis. And she was going to produce her own records, severing her production ties with Porter Wagoner.

Attacks from some of the old country guard were fierce and sometimes filled with venom. "Crucified" is the word Dolly likes to use about some of the nasty reactions to her new decisions.

"I don't like it when people say I fired my band. I did not fire my band. That was blown up by the press. But it was untrue and it hurt. My band was made up of my family, and I did not fire my family. My family and I are extremely close, and we always talk about the business and my plans and things—do now and did then.

"Some of my brothers and sisters were singers and players, and they just didn't like workin' the kind of schedule that I do. It was also takin' them away from their own writing. And their families and boy friends and girl friends. When you have to get on the road as much as I do, it's hard, and a lot of people just can't do it. So they knew I was goin' to make some changes, and they were glad about it actually.

"They trusted me to know it would work and they encouraged me. They wanted to get off on their own things, and they also knew I needed people that were more professional and things like that. Sometimes I know my music suffered because of poor sound and poor lightin' and things. And they knew that and understood that. They probably would have stayed on longer just to help

Nancy Barr

Dolly with her country music winners. From left: Johnny Wright and his wife Kitty Wells, Willie Nelson, Dolly, and Buck Trent.

me if I'd have needed them to or wanted them to. But I needed a band that was used to playin' material, very professional material, whether it's country or folk or rock music—anything I want to do. Some of them were qualified to do that and some were not, but they were all qualified in their own areas. And so nobody was fired. That's just not true.

"What is true is that I did make changes in my group. But they all knew that and we had discussed it over a long period of time. I told them I was disgusted with people who didn't know how to run my career, and we talked like family. They knew a lot of things I was gonna do, and they were more than willin' to give me a chance. And like I say, it gave them a chance to get back together. They weren't really that involved with country music or whatever, and it wouldn't have been fair to them to expect that. They were just younger and wanted to do their own things. That heavy grind really got to some of them.

"But it was kind of embarrassin' and hurt our feelin's a little bit when we'd see in a magazine that Dolly fired her family and things like that. That I'd changed and gone Hollywood. I realize that that's the kind of stuff you have to tolerate because that's the way the press will do it so it'll be more fascinatin' and sell more papers.

"I did not change. And I haven't gone Hollywood, although I don't really know what that means. I just wanted to bring my music to all different kinds of people. I'm lookin' for a new formula, one that doesn't have a label. I don't want to be classified as bein' country, pop, rock, or whatever. I just want to reach new people and do all kinds of things and cover new ground.

"I hate it when people say I've changed. Do I look like I've changed? Does singin' new kinds of songs mean I've changed? I had to try new things and broaden my audience. But I'm still the same Dolly Parton from the mountains, and I'll always be that. I'm not gonna turn my back on anybody ever. Tennessee is my home.

"You know when I first started doin' all this with the changes, a lot of people thought I was really crazy and screwin' up. They said I'd lose all my country fans and that I wouldn't get any new ones and I'd wind up with nothin'. They said my whole career was goin' to go down the drain. But I knew better. I knew I could do it. I just feel real confident. As far as entertainment goes, I don't think there's about anything I can't do. As long as it's right for me. And I'm not nearly what I know I'm gonna be. I like to think that I'm just startin' out really and climbin' higher all the time."

And she vows "I'm not gonna leave the country. I'd just like to take it with me wherever I go."

Over and over again Dolly stresses her need to do something extraordinary, something phenomenal, and her unfaltering belief that she can do just that. "I know I'm a big star already, but I want to be

Courtesy of Dolly Parton

more than that, more than even a superstar, I guess. Not because I am the greatest, but because I believe I have enough ability, personality, ambition, and determination and talent to get there."

The success and acclaim that greeted Dolly in her first crossover country-wide trip demonstrated that she was still the same shrewd old Dolly Parton as far as making career decisions. She was not only drawing the country stalwarts, but also new kinds of fans as well—hard rock aficionados, folk enthusiasts, even straitlaced Mantovani listeners flocked to her shows. Her audiences could not be pigeon-holed; they were totally diverse. She found that she had a large and loyal following among the gay crowd, that her flashy, flamboyant looks were as appealing to them as they were to the rednecks from the valleys. It was clear that Dolly was in no way alienating the old fans but just as she'd hoped, enlarging her fans and growing with them. Oh, at first, there would be some protests from country listeners who urged her against doing her new songs like "Here You Come Again." But gradually the country listeners became accustomed and decided they liked Dolly's music as much as ever.

Her shows went over particularly well in some of the rock-concert emporiums across the country like the Palladium and the Bottom Line in Manhattan, and the Boarding House in San Francisco. In mid-1977 she rejoiced that she was having more success in the first few months since her crossover than, she said, "in all the years that I've been killin' myself."

Her victory in the rock-music world was especially symbolized by her appearance in May 1977 at the Bottom Line. Such rock stars as Mick Jagger, Patti Smith, Bruce Springsteen, and pop artist Andy Warhol gathered to pay her tribute—first at the concert and then at a gala reception at Manhattan's plush Windows on the World, where she partied amid flowing champagne and five hundred guests. Dolly was a triumph, and she recalled, "I was a little bit nervous—on the brink of being scared. But when I walked out on stage I was at ease. The crowd was just great." Her entrance was met with cheers as she swept on stage in a gauzy, flowing gown, and at the finale, the audience gave her a fervent standing ovation.

Dolly Parton also scored high in such rock meccas as the Roxy on Sunset Strip in Los Angeles and at the Anaheim Convention Center in California.

In addition to her sell-out performances in the United States, Dolly also has entertained in Scotland, Germany, England, Holland, and Belgium. She sang for a Royal Jubilee TV special in London at the King's Theater, for which Queen Elizabeth was present. Later, Dolly, along with fellow performers Shari Lewis and David Soul, was introduced to the Queen and her husband, Prince Philip.

To document her entrance into the rarified and select world of superstardom, Dolly was profiled by such diverse publications as the prestigious *New York Times*, the rock bible *Rolling Stone*, *Good Housekeeping*, *People*, and *Playboy*, for which she posed dressed as a bunny. They all celebrated her enormous talent, but more than that, they enthused over Dolly's warm and loving and natural personality. As one interviewer complimented, "She's one of the most unshow-biz types of anyone I've ever met. She's as nice as she's cracked up to be."

Wide World Photos

Dolly, strumming on her banjo to sing "Applejack."

Overleaf: Dolly, denim-clad, rehearses for her debut at New York's Bottom Line club, in May, 1977.

Wide World Photos

UPI

Nancy Barr

Dolly, a favorite "Tonight Show" guest, chats with Johnny Carson.

Dolly also became a favorite of the talk-show circuit, her earthy humor and disarming honesty and quotable revelations livening up such shows as "Today," "Good Morning America," "Tonight," "Mike Douglas." Norman Lear placed a character in his soap opera take-off "Mary Hartman, Mary Hartman," who wanted to be a country-western singer and wear Dolly Parton-style outfits. The character was played by Mary Kaye Place, and Dolly was so delighted by the homage that she sang backup for Mary's debut record album.

Dolly's first album after her crossover, *New Harvest, First Gathering,* was released in March 1977. The title was probably suggestive of her attempts to assemble new material and new modes of expression in her music without losing her country base. In addition to the songs that Dolly wrote herself, she also presented interesting renditions in her light, shivery soprano of old standards like the soul classic "My Girl," sung by the Temptations; and others by Smoky Robinson and Jackie Wilson. The album, which Dolly personally produced with the help of Gregg Perry, her band leader and keyboard player, was not as successful as she had hoped. It garnered mixed reactions from the music critics and did not make the dent in the pop-music world that Dolly wanted. Although it was number one on the country charts, it never gained that all-important first position on the pop charts—which was what she was aiming for.

But Dolly learned something from that first album and applied the knowledge to her next album called *Here You Come Again* after her hit single of the same name. The album, which went gold and then platinum—the first in Dolly's career to do so—was "more smooth-sounding and pop" than she felt quite comfortable with, but she wanted to get the pop audience to listen to her.

As she told *Us* magazine, "When I did *Here You Come Again*, that was a special event. I was purposely tryin' to do somethin' to get myself established in the other field of music. And I knew what I'd done in the past wasn't what I needed to bridge that gap. So I just agreed, on the advice of my manager, to let them do the album, which they did. And it was platinum, and I can't argue with success. But that don't mean there aren't other ways to be successful."

As slick as *Here You Come Again* might have been, it did not turn off her country fans; it was the biggest country record she ever had.

She explains, "We used Gary Klein as the producer because he was havin' more hits than anyone else. And he did an excellent job. We were purposely tryin' to get an album and a single that would crossover and we did."

Here You Come Again was the first of Dolly's albums to be produced outside Nashville. The title song was written by the successful rock composers Barry Mann and Cynthia Weil, a team with many gold records under their belt. The LP was an interesting blend of rock, pop, and country, very different from Dolly's usual fare. Illustrative of its departure is the fact that the album contained only four songs composed by Parton herself. She drew upon material by John Sebastian and Kenny Rogers, among others.

Her latest album, *Heartbreaker*, has firmly established Dolly Parton in the mainstream of music. Released on RCA at the end of July 1978, the album became number one on the country charts in a few weeks and was rapidly climbing the pop charts. There was now no question that Dolly was as accepted and in demand in the pop-rocking sector as she was in the country realm.

The title song featured the tremulous Dolly vocalizing surrounded by some tangy piano accompaniment. Guitars and strings entered at crucial points throughout the song, which built to a strong finale. It was more of a pop-flavored tune, although not as slick as "Here You Come Again."

The album, which Dolly coproduced with Gary Klein—"I expect to go back to producin' my own, eventually," she says—featured ten songs, including six Parton originals. Although the album was heavy in pop idiom, there were unmistakable country strains and two vintage country songs, untouched by a pop influence. All the songs showed the unique Dolly singing to advantage. One of the songs, "Nickels and Dimes," was a poignant reminiscence about her girlhood, and this contrasted nicely with more aggressive and energetic numbers like "Baby I'm Burnin' " and "I Wanna Fall in Love."

As part of the RCA-planned promotion for the album, Dolly held a special free People's Concert on the steps of the New York City Hall on August 22. Dolly sang and told jokes and anecdotes about herself and answered questions from the crowd.

Dolly's newest project is an album with Linda Ronstadt and Emmylou Harris, both longtime and enthusiastic fans of the blond singer, even before she made her crossover. Emmylou Harris met Dolly when she came to Nashville, and then when Dolly was in Los Angeles, Emmylou invited Dolly to her house for tea. Later Emmylou introduced Dolly to Linda Ronstadt, who had been admiring Dolly's songwriting for years but had never met her. Dolly calls Linda "one of the greatest female voices I have ever heard."

UPI

After the three became friends, Dolly started working on a song called "Wildflowers" about three women. It was written with the three singers in mind, and when she told Ronstadt and Harris about it, the idea of a trio album emerged. Surrounded by the kind of secrecy befitting a CIA plot, the three met at Dolly's Nashville home in January 1978, where they worked on harmonies and chose songs for about four days. Initial recording was done in studios in Los Angeles, under the supervision of Emmylou's husband, Brian Ahern. Emmylou recalled that when she and Ronstadt were flagging in energy, it was Dolly with her indefatigable spirit who kept them going, while they were working almost the night through.

The album will have no one voice dominant on either side, but instead the three singers will trade off leads and harmonies. Dolly explains that the intensity of outside interest in the trio project has created a pressure on them to be especially careful on how they collaborate. They are also unsure of whether to give the album more of a rock sound or have more acoustic effects. Despite the problems, Dolly says, "It will be a shame to see the project end."

Dolly's not the first country performer to try to appeal to more citified listeners. The likes of Ronnie Milsap, Tammy Wynette, Loretta Lynn, and Conway Twitty have all attempted to lure pop fans into their corners, but none have enjoyed the kind of success Dolly has in widening her audience.

"I like to think my timing was right in crossing over," she explains. "I like to think I was the right type of person, that I was the right type of personality. I've also had a lot of good help from a lot of smart people. When I made the decision to do this because I knew I wanted to cover more ground, I just had to go to the right people. The ones I knew would help me accomplish this. Luckily I wound up with the right people that could dream as big as I was dreamin'.

"So it really worked out well. But I always thought it would. No matter what other people were sayin', I knew I could do it. And I think that sometimes if you just up and tell people what you want to do, I think it makes all the difference in the

Wide World Photos

Dolly, the queen of country, meets the Queen of England, Elizabeth II. With her are actress-puppeteer Shari Lewis and actor David Soul.

Courtesy of Dolly Parton

Dolly during a jam session with her two recording pals, Linda Ronstadt and Emmylou Harris. The trio is working on an album together.

world. They know better how to help you. So I went and said, I want to do this and this and this. And now it's all startin' to happen.

"I personally think the reason people love me is because I love them. And I think they know that. It's somethin' I share with everybody, not just country fans. I really do care about the people who are involved with me and who come to see my concerts. I appreciate my fans and their part in my career. It's somethin' that projects. If people treat you good and love you, then you love them back. That's the way I feel. I'm good to them because they're good to me. It's just a big mutual love. I want to make my fans happy, because then I make myself happy. It's what was in me all along, from when I was a kid, to love people and have them love you back. That's as much a part of my success as anything else."

Wide World Photos

Woman of Paradox

Dolly Parton is a curious fusion of contradictions. She is pure country, with that backwoods Tennessee drawl, yet she has a rapierlike intelligence and shrewdness that would impress the slickest of city dwellers. She has piled on artifice to the nth degree, with those mounds of wigs, bejeweled outfits, spike heels, and painted talons; yet, she seems, in spite of all those fake accoutrements, refreshingly natural and down-to-earth. The glittery paraphernalia may be fake but Dolly is not.

When you talk to her, she is almost disarmingly honest, never shying away from a difficult or tricky question. She's quick and witty, that basic intelligence apparent in the way she talks. Her conversation is full of eminently quotable stuff; without even trying she drawls pithy sayings that you know will become part of the lore of Dolly Parton. She giggles at herself, but she's also serio us and determined and comes across as a woman who is certain of what she wants and will get it. She can be at turns innocent and then the worldly-wise lady who jokes that if her bosom wasn't real she'd be the type to go out and have some made.

There's even a paradox in the way Dolly presents herself as a performer—that high-pitched girlish soprano swelling out of that voluptuous woman's body in red-hot-mama clothes.

There are no simple answers to what Dolly Parton is all about, and it's apparent that she likes it that way. "I like people to be curious about me, to be wonderin' about me," she admits with a coy laugh. "I'm even fascinatin' to myself. Life can get borin', so you have to spice it up and keep comin' up with surprises. I surprise myself every day. And I think that's good."

One of the things that Parton observers invariably wonder about is why she looks the way she does, why the makeup and the wigs and the flashiness? Some people have snickered over Dolly's appearance, but she claims that she's always had the last laugh. She regards it as a gimmick and one that has kept enough people intrigued for all the years she's been in show business. She doesn't dress that way out of any country ignorance; she does it on purpose. And whether her audiences laugh or are merely stunned by the rhinestone-studded razzmatazz, the effect is the same. They pay attention.

"My gaudy, artificial appearance has nothing to do with the kind of person I am. That's part of show business, and show business is a phony world anyway. So why not dress the part?

"I like to be different and I like people to pay

A meeting of two famous bodies. Dolly makes quite an armful for Arnold Schwarzenegger, body building champ.

attention. I just don't want to look like everybody else. I could be more stylish if I wanted to, but I'm not aimin' to be fashionable.

"My hair is out of the 1960s. My clothes are fifties. But nobody's goin' to change me. . . . I'm a kind of gaudy Liberace-type performer. I love my big hairdos. People are always pushin' me to change my look and I won't do it. It don't bother me. I like lookin' as if I came out of a fairy tale. I think it's funny for me. It's like I'm playin' out a fantasy that I had when I was a child, playin' with colors and flashy clothes.

"The glare and the glitter is a gimmick—fun for the audience, fun for me, something we can share together. The way I look really captures people's attention. . . . I look totally one way, but I am totally another. If people think I'm a dumb blond because of the way I look, then they're dumber than they think I am. If people think I'm not very deep because of my wigs and my outfits, then they're not very deep. I want people to like me, but if they can't see beyond all this, then that's their problem."

Gaudy, gimmick, and *extreme* are words that Dolly uses a lot to talk about her unusual appearance. It is as if she decided, instead of conforming to standard, to turn what was often the source of taunts and jests while she was growing up into a natural advantage in her career; if she were going to be extreme, she would capitalize on it. Dolly likes to be outrageous, and by all accounts her appearance has only enhanced her career. She has the courage to do what the rest of us only fantasize about—be different in the most bizarre way anyone can imagine—and she's loved all the more for it.

The artifice and the gaudiness are powerful magnets for Dolly to increase her appeal. She's often said, "If you have any talent, people are gonna overlook it, unless you've got something to get attention. The gimmick is the thing," she says, again showing that canny country shrewdness.

But her appearance is so extreme that it's often invited imitations. There are Dolly Parton look-alike contests with entrants in big wigs and flashy makeup and busty figures. It is easy to impersonate Dolly Parton; Vicki Lawrence stuck two balloons on her chest during a Carol Burnett show, donned a blond wig, and immediately became a Parton facsimile. Dolly says she gets a tickle out of all the contests and the parodies; after all, it makes people talk more and more about Dolly Parton.

Clearly, Dolly's happy with the way she is and plans to stay that way. She doesn't suffer from the typical performer's insecurity.

"I don't believe I am insecure in any way. I think I owe that to the way I was brought up and the way I was taught to have inner strength. It's an inner strength that comes from God, too.

"I think I'm as good as anybody else. I don't think I'm better than nobody. But I think I'm better than some people at other things. And I know I'm better at some things than I am at others. I just feel confident. I don't tackle things I don't know about or feel I couldn't do well. I just stay out of them. Stay away from the areas that I know I'm not qualified in. So therefore I don't have to be insecure. I know what I can do and I know what I can't do. Nobody else is gonna figure that out for you but you yourself."

Dolly's so secure that she can poke fun at aspects of herself other people might feel insecure about. She likes to make jokes about her figure, claiming that if she took up jogging, "I would give myself two black eyes for a couple of good reasons." There's a long-running Dolly Parton gag that when she burned her bra it took the fire department days to put out the blaze, and Dolly may have started the joke herself. When she performed in concert in Sevier County on behalf of the annual Dolly Parton Scholarship Fund (she had the fund started for the high school she was graduated from in 1964), she teased, "I see some of you out there have binoculars. I know what you're lookin' at. You're tryin' to see if they're as big as they say they are." Then after one of those classic pregnant pauses, she said with a mischievous chuckle, "I'm talking about my wigs."

Two frequent questions asked of Dolly are her measurements and whether she's had any artificial help with her figure. She's never disclosed her measurements and says she doesn't plan to. All she says is just that when she eats a lot, she is 80-80-80.

About whether all of Dolly is natural, she says, "It doesn't matter what I say. People are going to believe what they want. It's just another thing to keep people wonderin' and guessin', so let them do that," she laughs.

She asserts that she's not really sensitive about any kind of talk or jokes about her figure. "Only if it's really vulgar, to the point where it's embarrassin'. After all, you can't ignore the fact that it's there, that my bosom's there. If it's in good taste and just playful, it don't bother me at all. I just don't like tacky jokes about myself or anybody else. I

Courtesy of Dolly Parton

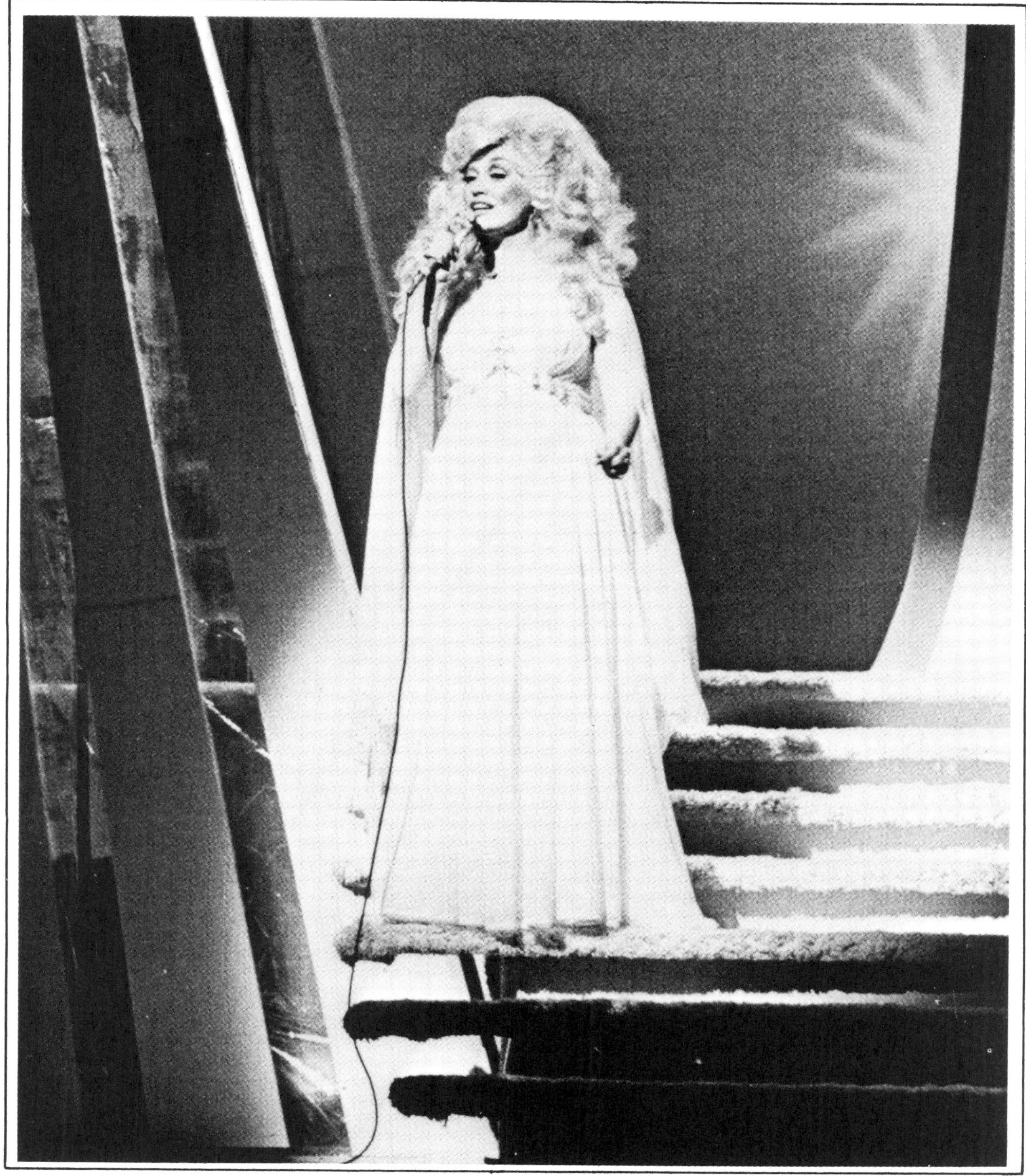

don't like somebody to be downright tacky. You know, I'm just a big person. If you pardon the expression, that's what I've always called myself, a big person. When I was younger it was more embarrassing. But I can't be too sensitive about them; they've made me rich."

Dolly has a kind of infectious sunny optimism about her, which is surprising for someone in the field of show business. People come away from one meeting with Dolly Parton invariably saying that she is one of the nicesı women they have ever met. To know Dolly is to fall in love with her warm, bubbly, perky personality. Sure she's been disappointed, felt pain and hurt, but with Dolly the scars have healed over with the force of her buoyant cheerfulness.

Linda Ronstadt once remarked about her: "I've never met anyone so free of neurosis as that person. . . . She's just kind of a Southern magnolia blossom that floats on the breeze. But she's no dummy."

Dolly claims not to get into moods or big depressions, like many performers. She describes herself as being very sentimental, capable of being touched by something very simple, and also being very emotional. But she's not the type to go into black, dour states.

"I got my feet planted firmly on the ground. I know what's right for me. And I know what's best for me. I just love life. I'm excited about all the things that are happenin' now and about all the things I'm thinkin' about and plannin' for the future.

"I wouldn't tell somebody else how to run their life, and by the same token, I don't want anybody tellin' me how to run mine. I'll listen to good advice and I'll use it when I can, but I know in my own heart what I should and shouldn't do. I just think everything is in good shape and in good order now."

And part of the reason for her shipshape life is her faith in God, she believes. Dolly and Carl do not go to church anymore, but she calls herself a religious person. She also calls herself a "vanilla sinner," a curious phrase of her own concoction, which means, she says that she's a combination of both bad and good.

"I'm extremely religious. I'll always be that way. But I don't claim to be a Christian. And that's because I don't want to set a bad example. I've often said that I'm too good to be bad and too bad to be good, and I really mean that 'cause I don't want people to think I'm the one to follow. If I set an example at all, I just want people to know that I acknowledge God and I know God no matter what I do.

"I believe that all good things come from God. I think that if my work has touched people at all, it's because of God. I just think that nothin' good can come from evil, so I like to think my success is because of the good there is in me. That's got a lot to do with my attitude and my feelin', like I say, of inner strength.

"I pray every day. Normally I don't get down on my knees or anythin' but it's just in my mind. Sometimes I do get down on my knees if I feel it's necessary to pray about something that's really sincere or whatever.

"But I don't claim to be anything at all. But I do believe and I have been saved and baptized. Religion is just somethin' very serious to me.

"I don't always do the right thing, but I always know when I'm doin' somethin' wrong and it's not the right thing. But it don't bother me; I don't trouble myself about it. God gives me a well of strength. I know He is there no matter what I do. Mistakes I make are not His fault; they're just my own. But He gives me courage and He helps me. I'm not afraid of God; I can joke with him. But He's very important in my life, although I don't call myself any kind of fanatic.

"I think that's one of the greatest things about my success and about my attitude and the fact that I can hold it all together. I know I've got help whenever everybody else might seem not to be there for me. I always know that God is there. And I can talk to Him and always seem to feel better and know the right answers.

"I never make a decision about business or anything without talkin' to God about it, and usually when I do, I feel after I pray that I've got my answer."

Freedom means a lot to Dolly Parton, freedom to believe as she wishes, dress the way she wants, and climb as far in her career as she can. She's firm in her idea of who she is and what she wants, unshakable in her perception of her goals and image. She's ferociously independent and speaks of herself as being as stubborn as a mule, unwilling to be swayed by other people or manipulated.

"I don't consider myself a rebel so much as I aim to do as I please. . . . I ain't got time to worry about whether people are resenting me or not, because I'm too busy tryin' to make somethin' out of myself and to make life worth somethin' I can leave behind for somebody else to study and analyze when I'm gone."

Sometimes she says she feels like she is a loner today, not because of lack of friends, but because "I'm just such an individual. I'm very close to people so I don't feel lonely. There's a big difference between the two. And I feel very independent. I feel I can make it under any conditions because of the way I am. I feel like I would know what to do in any situation.

"I have lots of friends, lots of close friends, and all that. I feel like I belong now and I feel like I have a place, and the reason that I was misunderstood in the beginning of my life is all gone. But I'm still real different."

Although Dolly appears quite pleased and happy about her success, she claims it is not much of a surprise to her. One way or another, she says, she always knew that it would happen. "I've got confidence and I've got guts," she says with emphasis. It is all part of the Parton positive thinking philosophy. She is a passionate believer in willing and dreaming yourself to be anything you want to be. There is a kind of religious quality about her positive thinking, probably born out of that fundamentalist religion background.

"You know," she exhorts, "you can think yourself rich or you can think yourself poor. You can think yourself havin' a horrible marriage or you can make it work. If you're sick, you can think yourself well.

"Even before I knew they wrote books on positive thinkin', I grew up where faith was what carried us through—you know, faith healin' and that sort of thing.

"So I thought, 'I want myself to be happy. I like myself. I'm all I've got. So why can't I have the best for myself?' "

The urge to believe, Dolly claims, is what got her out of that poor wooden shack and made her into a millionaire singer. She has said that the goals she set for herself years ago, in elaborate lists, have come true to a large extent. She confides that many of the things that she wrote down long ago have been realized and come true, just like she believed they would. "Positive thinkin' is a marvelous thing," she says.

So marvelous that Dolly is today not only one of the country's top performers and most exciting personalities but also a very rich woman. She has an assortment of investments, tax shelters, and businesses that amount to well over a million dollars. She owns three publishing companies, including one called Velvet Apple, the controlling interest in Owepar, and Nashville's Fireside Studios. She owns the company that makes the popular Dolly doll, and she would like to market a line of her wigs. Yet she's no arriviste spendthrift. "I don't spend that much money on myself these days," she admits, " 'cause I never have time to shop. But being brought up poor you always appreciate the value of a dollar. You never spend a lot of money on something without thinking about it. That don't mean you don't spend the money. But you do it with thought. I'm glad that I can spend now and have the things that I want and I need. If I wanted something, I would go and get it, but usually I like for other people to have nice things, like my family."

Besides being good to her family, Dolly is also quite close with her band. She doesn't pull any star stuff but will eat at the counter in coffeehouses and diners with the crew. She remembers their names, all of them, jokes with them, asks them about their loved ones. She is like a big mother hen.

"I don't consider myself a hard person to work for. But I'm tricky. I'm not hard to work for at all; in fact, I'll give you every freedom, every chance in the world to do your job. But if you can't do the job, then I won't quarrel with you and I won't argue with you. That's not what I do with musicians. I'll treat you good as long as I think what you're doin' is right musically. If I feel it's not right musically, then I'll go to the person and say that I have to make some changes. But I never argue and fight. I'm not temperamental like that.

Dolly at the Country Music Awards in California in 1977—as glittering as ever.

Wide World Photos

Nancy Barr

Left: Dolly strikes a poignant note while singing one of her latest hits, "Heartbreaker."

Below: Dolly and friends outside the custom-built bus that takes her all over the country on singing tours.

Nancy Barr

"I'm really friends with all the people I work with. I don't consider myself above them because I'm the star. I love those people. They're handpicked. They're people that I feel extremely close to. I don't travel separate from them; I don't stay in separate hotels or anything like that. I travel with them. We need each other to survive. We are all makin' a living for each other. The kind of schedules and commitments I have I would have to be close to the people I work with. And as long as they do their job and do what they have to do onstage, that's what counts.

"If somebody's got the potential to do a job and then they don't, then that makes me extremely mad. If I know a person's not capable, then I'll just go as far as I can with them, but if they are capable then they have to perform."

Dolly is also especially attentive to her fans; often after concerts she will stand outside and seemingly endlessly sign autographs for the people who want them, and will do it until they've all gone home, happy with her fancy-dancy signature and the memory of that glittery smile.

"I think my fans know how much I care about them and appreciate them. I appreciate even the slightest little thing like buying a ticket or carin' enough to write a letter. The only way I can pay them back is to treat 'em real good, at least the best I can and try to give them as much as I can on the stage and on TV.

"I need all the help and support I can get because I want to accomplish a lot of things. I want to make them happy and make myself happy. And that's the best way to do it."

To make them happy Dolly travels in her custom-made bus as much as 150,000 miles a year and sometimes as much as three hundred days of that year, rolling on the highways at night while other people are fast asleep in stationary homes. On a tour that will take her from such far-flung places as Sioux City, Iowa, to Hickory, North Carolina, and even to New York City, she will often wake up in a different town every day. But Dolly claims the traveling does not bother her that much.

"I get kinda restless if I stay in one place too long. I like to go home, of course, but then I like to get back on the road and back to my music. It's a gypsy feeling that I have. And it's also fascinatin', to me, to meet new people and see all kinds of places. You have to remember that growin' up in the mountains as I did, you just stay in the same place and that can be borin'. So I know it's hard and some people couldn't take it at all but I like it."

Unlike other country entertainers, Dolly does not travel in a separate bus from her band and crew members. They all travel together, which is the way she likes it, because "the people that I work with are like my family."

The bus is equipped with a color TV, a CB radio, a kitchen, two bathrooms, and eleven beds. Dolly has her own tiny bedroom, with a couch and a large bed that comes out to take up almost the full room when she sleeps. There are three closets in the room, one for just her stage clothes and cabinets for her wigs with stands to hold each one. She usually takes along twenty-five to thirty wigs for a month-long tour, "about a wig a day," and if she'll be on the road longer than that, Dolly will pack some wigs in the extra room in the luggage department underneath the passenger area—specially designed for her wigs.

That bus with all its special equipment and gear is a way of life she probably knows better now than any other. "I spend ninety percent of my time on the bus," she declares. "I've been in show business about fourteen years, and I've always traveled on custom buses."

Wearing those curlicued platinum blond wigs also has become a way of life for Dolly Parton. Actually, she says that she has been wearing wigs for about five years, since she was in her late twenties. Before that, she used to tease up her own hair.

"I love to tease up my hair. I remember when I was about fifteen, everybody was teasin' up their hair and I always liked to see how high and puffy I could make it. I used to love to bleach and tease my hair and have this big-haired image.

"When my hairstyle went out of style I decided that I would keep it anyway. Because I liked it and I knew that it would get attention. I just like the way it looks on me. And I'm only a small person, only five feet. So I wear a lotta hair, with it piled up high to offset that." Dolly likes to tease that her real height is five feet but with wigs and heels she's six feet four inches.

"I decided I would use wigs for convenience. That way I wouldn't have to carry somebody on the road with me to do my hair. I could have the wigs preset, and since they're synthetic, they won't lose their curl like human hair does."

When she's traveling on her bus, often she doesn't wear a wig. She just pulls her own hair back and puts on a scarf. Another aspect of the Dolly Parton mythology is that no one has ever seen her

Courtesy of Dolly Parton

Dolly's curly, mountainous hairstyles have become her trademark.

own hair, but she denies this. Among the people who have seen Dolly without a wig are other country performers like Loretta Lynn and of course her family.

"My real hair is blond and baby fine. And I bleach it so that it stays blond.

"I was a white-headed child. My hair always was blond, real blond, until I was half-grown. Then it started gettin' that dingy lookin' blond, sort of a mousy blond like most blond people get when their hair starts gettin' darker. It never gets brown, but it doesn't stay blond. . . . I'm sure it would be a dark shade of blond if it really grew out now, but it wouldn't be a color I'd be happy with."

Dolly used to wear her hair shoulder length, but now she has cut it to about a chin length, less Mae West in look and more Marilyn Monroe. And she's switched to shorter wigs to go along with her haircut.

She vows that someday she'll go back to wearing her own hair, but that probably won't be for a long time. "When the public knows me, when I become as successful as I want to be, when I get established really well, then I can do whatever I want. When I become the universal star and superstar that I want to be, then you can look and be any way you want because if you've got the ambition and the talent and the guts, it don't matter what you look like."

As much as her hairstyle is a throwback to her youth, so is Dolly's choice of wardrobe. The towering, spindly heels and the slinky outfits in shiny, glitsy fabrics recall the times when lascivious blonds like Jayne Mansfield and Marilyn Monroe were undulating across the screen during the late fifties and early sixties, when straight skirts and figure-hugging clothes were in. Dolly loves clothes; she has closets full in her Nashville home, and an entire wing is packed with her stage costumes and more casual wear. And she has a special fondness for shoes, the kind of old-fashioned high heels that, like the wigs, give her the inches she always longed for longitudinally.

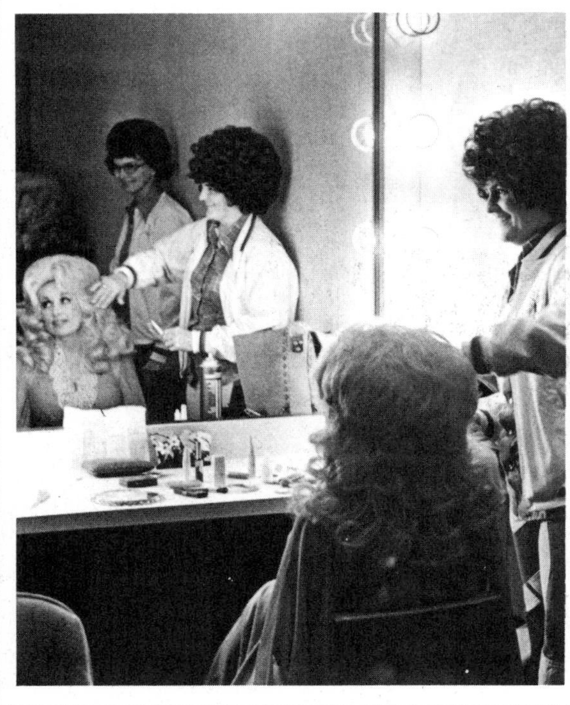

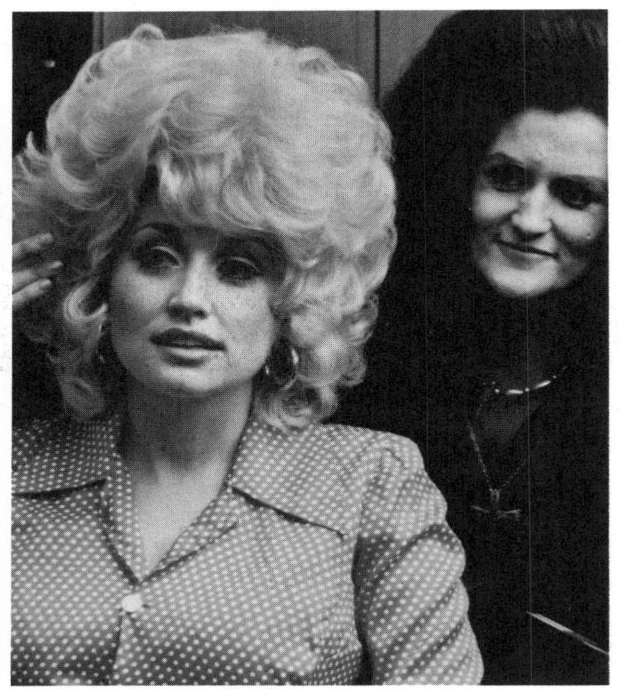

Mike Borum

"I still like the pointed toes and the spike heels. They impressed me so when I was a kid. I buy thousands of dollars of shoes every year."

Most of her shoes Dolly buys at the famed emporium of sexy couture, Frederick's of Hollywood, where the shoes are high and sexy and vampy like she likes them. But contrary to popular opinion, Dolly does not buy Frederick's clothes because she confesses she cannot buy clothes off a rack. "I'm hard to fit, because of my proportions, so I have my things specially made."

Dolly works with a hairdresser to achieve just the right look for her hairstyle.

Courtesy of Dolly Parton

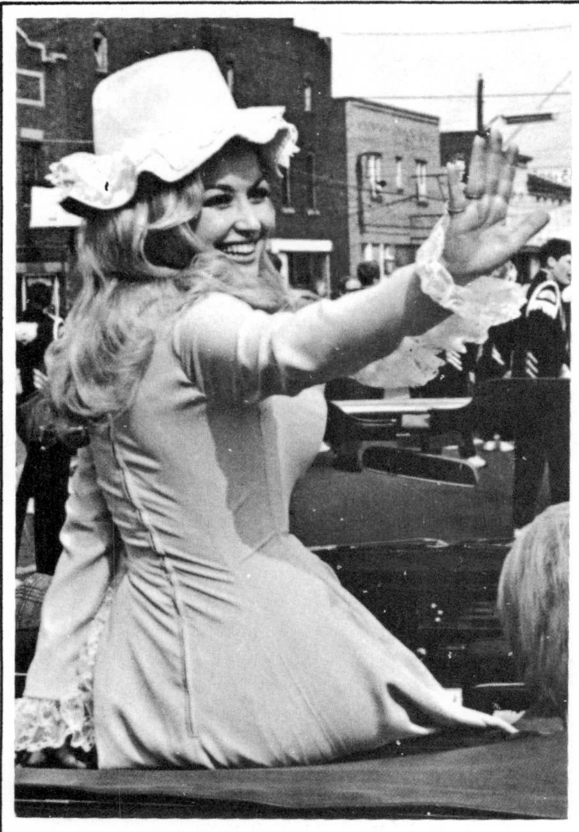

Dolly returns home for Dolly Parton Day in Sevierville, Tennessee.

She prefers her stage clothes to be hand washable so she can rinse them out in a motel-room sink. She likes clothes that are wrinkle free because she says she doesn't have to iron them and she doesn't have to worry about dry cleaning. As Dolly says, in her way of remarking on the small conveniences in life, "We're so lucky being in a country where there are all these beautiful fabrics which are washable."

Despite the quintessential hourglass figure and the tight costumes, Dolly insists that she doesn't envision herself as sexy.

"I don't think of myself as a sex symbol. I'm more of a character and a personality. Besides, I don't want the responsibility of thinking about what I look like and what I weigh. I don't want to have to be a beautiful woman and have to worry if I put on ten pounds or somethin' like that.

"I want to be thought of as somebody different and somebody special—but not special to look at. I want to be more than that. I have a lot of depth and while these kinds of clothes are my trademark, there's more to me than that. My fans know that."

Her fans and admirers also know that Dolly is a surprising woman, always coming up with startling revelations about herself and her life. She's a remarkably intelligent person with a no-nonsense country wisdom, yet she admits that she doesn't read much and has little time to be interested in politics and who is running for what. She may joke about her bosom, but she describes herself as a very modest person who does not like to dress or undress in front of other people or wear body-baring clothes. She is one of the celebrity world's richest entertainers, commanding tens of thousands of dollars a night in concert fees, yet she is one of the least affected and most natural of women, one who still likes playing horseshoes and cooking turnip greens and meat loaf and claims potatoes and junk food are her favorites. She talks about how important freedom is to her, and in all respects is a modern kind of woman, but she says that she cannot keep up with the women's movement and that she would never call herself a feminist.

"I don't even understand that women's liberation stuff, don't know what it's all about. I'm a lucky person. I'm liberated, free-spirited, free-minded, but it's not something I promote or push—just a natural way I've always lived."

Perhaps one of the most revealing things about Dolly Parton was unearthed during her television interview with Barbara Walters. Barbara told Dolly that in spite of the many differences between them—Barbara Walters is a New York-bred Jewish sophisticate who is about as conservative looking as Dolly is outrageous looking—she felt that in many ways, underneath the obvious differences, they were alike. Dolly agreed and said that she felt she could relate to her interviewer a lot.

"There's the drive," she told Barbara Walters. "I think we're both very positive. We're both positive and we're both determined and stubborn about the things we believe in."

Perhaps that's why Dolly Parton from the Smoky Mountains has such universal appeal. There's something in her complicated and outrageously adorned package for everyone. She once said, "People don't come to see you be you. They come to see you be them." Dolly, the creator and creature of fantasy, seems to make anyone's fantasy appear possible. She is a country woman who speaks to everyone, whether they live on crowded city streets or in lonely backwoods valleys.

"I have a communication with people, and I can project to them and they can detect a sincerity and honesty in what I'm sayin' to them because I mean what I say to the audience. I'm tellin' their stories.

"We are all made up of the same things. . . . a heart, a soul, and feelings. We want to be important and noticed, to be pleased and satisfied. We all have mothers and daddies and family problems. A lot of songs I write about, talk about just ordinary things. And I think the basic simplicity of my music attracts a lot of people. It's simple, yet it says a lot."

No matter how much Dolly Parton's wealth and popularity may have increased over the past few years or how much they will increase in the future, she declares that at heart she will always be the same woman with the country spirit and soul.

"Attention ain't affectin' me. My life's just like it was when I started out," she maintains. She may be a big Hollywood star, but Dolly Parton is not planning to forsake her Nashville roots and pull up stakes and settle in California.

As she once said, "I could sit there on the corner of Hollywood Boulevard and watch those freaks forever. I love to go there.

"But you see I grew up in the country where life was simple and easy and you had the time to know and love your neighbors and I would miss that a lot."

UPI

Dolly at Home

Dolly Parton's marriage to Carl Dean, four years her senior, strikes many observers as a puzzlement. Here is a woman who is a gregarious and outgoing entertainer, a bouncy type who talks about everything from sex to family health matters honestly and openly; yet her husband is reclusive and leads a life shrouded in secrecy. The figure of Carl Dean is such a mysterious one that people have joked, even to Dolly herself, that perhaps he is just a fantasy creature, made up from the blond singer's creative imagination.

Dolly and Carl have been married over twelve years, since their small wedding in Nashville on May 30, 1966. During that time, despite the fact that Dolly's prominence has been enhanced each year and mushroomed in a Kleig-light atmosphere, Carl remains a retiring and reserved type, completely loath to seek publicity. He is rarely photographed and never interviewed. Carl Dean keeps a mighty low profile, working on the farm around the Taralike mansion he shares with Dolly in Nashville and runnng his own asphalt paving company. Although Dolly has enough money and enough handsome investments to keep the two of them cozy for years, he still enjoys working at his trade. Sometimes he'll grade a driveway or clean off some property for a few hundred dollars—a fraction of the amount Dolly receives for one concert. He is his own man, and as Dolly once said, "He don't want people to stare and point at him to say 'There's Dolly Parton's husband.' He don't want to have that kind of publicity, and he doesn't need it." And he could not be further divorced from Dolly's career, taking no part in her management or her plans whatsoever.

Dolly and Carl are happily married, a rarity among couples and rarer still among the marital strife of show business. But talk about their curious marriage and unconventional arrangement persists and Dolly admits sometimes it gets to her.

"I guess it really don't bother me," she says, "it's just that you get tired of answering the same old questions about it. We are together more than most people think, more than those stories which say that we only see each other about six weeks a year. That's just a bunch of junk you read in the papers and the magazines. We're together more than I ever talk about; he joins me on the road a lot. Either I'll go to see him in the midst of a tour, or else I'll call and tell him to come on up to where I'm playing. And he does, but we don't like a lot of publicity about it when he does.

"We actually are together as much as we need to be together. We know how much we need to be together and nobody else does. We know what is best for us. Ain't nothin' nobody could say that could change that, or anybody's criticism or won-

Courtesy of Dolly Parton

derin' about our marriage. If it's necessary, we'll be together. We're free and we don't have children.

"If I get lonesome, I call and say come on out here, or I will cancel if I really need to go home. I'll reschedule something. So I don't feel like I'm trapped or anything. I don't feel like I have to do anything if I need to see Carl. I don't have to work dates I've got—I will because I'm a very responsible person—but if I want to go home I can. If there are health problems or personal problems or family problems, I will go home. Or if it's necessary for my mind to relax or somethin'. I'm very close to my family, so I would just go home and be with Carl and with my relatives, especially if there is some kind of problem.

"He's nothin' like what people might think. He wants to be an ordinary person, and he is, but it's in an extraordinary way. He's real smart, one of the smartest men I ever met—he's got lots of what we call horse sense. And he's also really funny and witty. He's got a kind of earthy sense of humor like mine, which is good. We make each other laugh."

Dolly once told how Carl joked about how he would like to relieve himself "in the chimney corner" but was afraid some fan would take his photograph while he was doing it.

"He's very independent and strongminded. He's his own person. And he's a private person. He reminds me a lot of my daddy, probably more than anything else. And I respect my daddy a lot."

That's probably why Dolly calls her husband Daddy. She says that he hates for her to call him Carl. And the same is true for her. Carl never calls his wife Dolly. Instead he'll say, "the old woman" or "crazy woman." Dolly admits that if he did use her proper name that her feelings would be hurt and she wouldn't like it.

Dolly says that Carl is like her little boy, like her brother, like her daddy, all rolled into one person. "We're the best of friends," she enthuses, and adds, "I know I'm like a mother and sister and little girl to him.

"Our marriage is perfect in every way. Perfect for him, perfect for me. Carl and I have never had an argument. He is one of my favorite people and he would be that even if we weren't married. But I know we'll always be together. There's no way I would ever leave him. If I fell in love with another man? Well, that wouldn't happen. I would avoid that. I might be drawn to somebody else, even in a powerful sort of way, but I know what I have with Carl. What we have together is so good and so sweet that I'd never want it to get messed up. . . .I wouldn't want to 'learn' another man the way I've 'learned' Carl."

Dolly confesses that she and Carl are not jealous kinds of people. And she's frank enough to admit that if either one of them had an affair, it would not mean the end of a marriage. What they probably would do is just not let the other person know. She says there could be temptations for both of them, but that neither would let anything happen to their marriage.

As Dolly told Barbara Walters in a special television interview, "He's the kind of person that if bein' apart, if we should meet somebody I would never tell him. He would never know and I would never tell him. And it wouldn't hurt him. It's the same way with him. I wouldn't want to know it. As long as he loves me and as long as he's good to me and as long as we're good to each other. I don't think it happens, but I'm just sayin' I wouldn't want to pry in it."

And Dolly has said that she is the kind of strong-willed person that if she wanted to have an affair she would. And it would not involve anybody else, even Carl, except for her and the other man. But she vows, no matter what, "Nobody could ever take the place of Carl. We both know that we are here to stay."

What does he give her, this man whom Dolly sees so comparatively little yet loves so much? "He gives me everything," she says a bit breathlessly. "Just everything. He gives me love and understanding and kindness and thoughtfulness. And he gives me freedom, which is something I give him as well. We don't talk about it or think that one day we'll give each other freedom. It's not that kind of thing. He just likes me to be the way I am, and he wants me to stay the way I am. And in order for me to be the way I am, I have to be free to be that. I have to go travelin' and do my singin' and work on my career. Carl understands all that. And he gives me roots. And we share things together, even the simplest little things. We have a great amount of happiness in our marriage."

Initially, when Dolly was a fledgling singer in Nashville, she thought she would never get married. Not that no one would ever ask, but that no man would want to be married to a woman who never intended to marry and settle down and have children, but who wanted to roam the world for weeks at a time, in search of some large dreams. "No, I didn't plan on gettin' married," she ac-

knowledges. "But meetin' Carl changed all that. I knew he would never ask me to quit or give it up; he knows what is important to me."

Actually, she says that her long-distance marriage is the best for both of them; it really would not work better any other way, she claims. "We're both independent-type people; we both do our things. Sometimes when I get home, after a while, I start itchin' to get back on the road again and do my music. By now we're accustomed to our lives and we like it that way."

Unlike other show-business marriages, especially in the realm of country music where Tammy Wynette was guided by her former husband George Jones, and Loretta Lynn's husband, Mooney, advises her, the marriage of Dolly Parton and Carl Dean does not mix career and love.

"I know I wouldn't like a man who got really involved with my career. My nerves couldn't stand that, and I got nerves of steel. I don't know how people in the business deal with a husband runnin' their careers. I'm just not criticizin' it; I just don't know how they do it.

"Even the simplest little things get on your nerves if you're together all the time. Much less if your husband is tryin' to tell you how to run your business. It's just more trouble on top of your personal problems and things. It does seem to work well for some people, but I couldn't put up with it. He never gets involved with my business. That's why I hire people to take care of it. I wouldn't want to be in business with Carl, and I love him more than anything. I just wouldn't want to take the risk of there bein' any problems.

"Carl's an honest and decent and good man, and we have an honest and good relationship. I wouldn't want to screw it up with all this business stuff."

Besides, as Dolly has said, asserting her strong-willed attitude, "I need my husband for love and other men for my work. But I don't depend on any man for my strength."

Carl remains so separate from Dolly's music that there was talk that he had never seen her perform. It was one of those homegrown Nashville tales that

Dolly with Cher on a television special. Unlike Dolly, Cher does mix her career and love life.

Nancy Barr

was circulated through the music industry and came to be accepted as part of the lore of Dolly Parton.

"That was just a joke," she says. "It was one of those exaggerations. He didn't used to like my singin' all that much, but he likes it a lot better now. He likes my new album a lot, *Heartbreaker,* and the new kinds of music I'm doin'.

"He doesn't particularly care for country music. What he likes is hard rock and bluegrass. He just never was into the music I was doin' before, especially when I was doin' the real country thing. But now he likes some of the things I'm doin', and that means a lot. I'm glad he's a real big fan of mine now."

Carl likes to tease Dolly. Once, after seeing her perform at a concert in Louisville, Kentucky, he came backstage to congratulate her and told her that if she kept at it, she might be somebody someday. And if people talk to him about being Dolly Parton's husband, he is likely to roar, good-naturedly, "Hell, she ain't makin' no money."

Dolly and Carl have no children now, and she doubts that she will ever have any. But that is one thing she talked to Carl about before they were married, about the demands of her career.

"I might have children someday, but I don't really think so," she says. "I raised enough of my brothers and sisters so I was like a second mama to them, and it made me feel like a mother. Besides, I don't think it's fair to be on the road all the time like I am and have kids. I couldn't bear the thought of havin' someone else take care of them and bein' away from them for weeks at a time. I love children a lot, but I don't think it would be fair to them or fair to me to do both.

"Carl and me helped raise some of my brothers and sisters in our home in Nashville. The last of them just got married several months ago, so I don't have any kids right now. And I don't miss that. I enjoy havin' the freedom to do what I want and so does Carl. I feel like I've been raisin' babies all my life. And this is the first time in all our twelve years of marriage that Carl and I've been really alone. It's like we're on a second honeymoon, when all the kids have grown up and gone off to be married. We're really havin' a good time now.

"There's always kids around the house, what with my brothers and sisters havin' their own families. I'm extremely close to my family, and when we all get together, there's plenty of kids. So I can't say that I miss havin' my own kids.

"If later on Carl and I decide we want to have children, and I'm naturally too old to have them, then we can adopt some. Meanwhile, I feel like my music and my songs are my children. That's what I've created and that's what'll last for me when I'm gettin' on in years.

"Carl and I feel like we've raised a big family between us, and now we're on our own. So we're just gonna enjoy ourselves and do the things we want to do."

Dolly and Carl, in their precious moments of togetherness, share the good life; but it is also a quiet life and a simple life.

"In what little time we have together, we'll just do simple things," confides Dolly. "Nothin' fancy or special. Like I'll cook the things he likes. He likes roast beef and green beans and hearty-style food.

"I'm a good cook, a real good cook, but I don't cook any exotic things. But what I cook, I cook well because I'm a good eater and I'm a big eater. All the things I like are fattening. So if I think it tastes good, then it's good. Carl thinks I'm a good cook, too. I'm a real creative cook since I don't go by a recipe. I make up a lot of stuff. I cook like my mother, just kinda makin' it up as I go along. I seem to know what tastes good.

"We don't talk about music or business. We talk about the family or about our house or somethin' to do with the farm. We like to take walks together and go on picnics or else just sit outside on the porch.

"We're not much for entertainin' a lot or big socializin', things like that. We do have our families over a lot and our friends. But nothin' on a big scale. We don't have big fancy parties or things like that. And I don't really hang out with other country-music folks. When I get home, I love to be at home and then I like to rest and not go rushing around crazy. Sometimes when I'm home more than a few weeks straight, I get restless and bored. Then I want to get back on my bus and go out again on the road and Carl likes that, too, for me to be gone."

Dolly's parents live in a house she bought for them not far away, but there is a roomy mobile home camped near the Porter-Dean mansion for her folks to stay when they visit. She says that as her father gets on in years, he is less likely to take trips from home, but Dolly's mama visits all the time. And during holidays, like Thanksgiving and Christmas, Partons and Owenses gather from far and wide for an old-fashioned family dinner.

Dolly rarely gets to take a vacation, but when she

does it is a modest one with Carl. Just a few years back the couple went out West in the family station wagon. They camped out in Yellowstone National Park. And when they are together Dolly says she does not wear one of her famous wigs. She just lets her real hair, which is a blond shade, go natural, sometimes tucked under a bandana.

Although, if you counted hours, Dolly's real home would be the bus she travels all over the country on with her band; she loves her house just outside Nashville. It was important for her to have, this mansion, as a symbol of her success and the long road she has traveled since her birth in a cabin in Sevier County.

"I really like havin' a nice house," she says proudly. "That was important to me. We had it built even before I could really afford it, but it was my dream house and it still is. And I'm decoratin' it like a dream house."

It has twenty-three rooms plus lots of walk-in closets and bathrooms. The house, which Carl helped to build, is very elegant looking, with six stately pillars adorning the front and upper and lower story verandas. It is a perfect image of a *Gone With the Wind* type estate, the kind of place a Southern belle like Dolly would dream about.

But it is also a cozy home for family relatives and not intimidating at all. Carl has joked that the colonial-style house is the Parton hotel; Dolly chuckled that it was like a "depot." She also teases that she and Carl have a credit card sign up as a joke and that they are sure to accept all of them if you visit.

A two-hundred-acre farm surrounds the house, which is in the horse country outside Nashville. There's a stable of horses, twenty-five polled Hereford cows, peacocks that strut on the lawn, and some dogs. Every room in the house has a closet, and they're all large. The size of the closet in Dolly's bedroom is about that of a small room. She keeps her clothes organized according to category, throughout the closets, with her skirts, dresses, and jeans upstairs and her winter coats and costumes—about three thousand glittery, rhinestone-covered "work outfits," as Dolly calls them—downstairs.

The kitchen, where Dolly does her home-style cooking, is one room she's especially fond of. It is the only room without a closet, too. It is double sized and equipped with both modern appliances and an old wood-burning stove, like the one her mother used.

The house, surrounded as it is by so much farmland, is set back from the highway by several miles. A creek snakes through their property, too. Since Dolly describes both herself and Carl as loners in a way, especially when she comes home to rest after a tour, they both like to sit outside in rockers on the porch and talk. "I think this gives me a contentedness that audiences can sense wherever I go. It's my foundation, havin' that house and Carl there; those are my roots,." she says.

Dolly's youngest sister, Rachel, was the Parton sibling who probably spent the most time at the mansion. She lived with Carl and Dolly until recently and went to high school in Nashville. But some of the other Parton brood, including Cassie, Randy, and the twins, Floyd and Frieda, all stayed there from time to time, especially during the summers.

"When you're born and raised in the country like I am," Dolly explains, "you always share what you have. We were poor when we were younger, and we all shared in that. Now that I'm rich and makin' good money, it's like we're all rich. And we all share in the good times and the happiness it has brought, and we're all thankful for it."

And many of the good times for Dolly and her large brood of relatives—there is speculation that thousands, or at least hundreds, of Dolly's kin live in the mountain area around Nashville—take place in her dream house. (Carl and Dolly also own a house in the fancy Belle Meade section of Nashville and she rents a plain apartment in Los Angeles when she's out in Hollywood, but the white-pillared house is what they really call home.)

Much of the reason why Dolly holds so much affection for this place is that Carl, along with her uncle, built it up "board by board," as she says. It took the two men almost two years to do it, and Dolly describes that "you never saw anybody work harder at anything." She recalls how when she finished a tour, it was exciting for her to come back and see how the house-building was progressing, how everything was taking shape as the months went by.

Of course, Dolly and Carl could have had a builder do it, someone to carry out their dreams. But Dolly confides that Carl wanted to do it himself, and it was kind of a tribute of his love to her that he did and worked so hard at it. And his building that house to her she says was the most wonderful gift in the world, better than anything he could have bought. There are special touches that he added

Globe Photos

A front view of the dream house that Carl helped build for Dolly, the Tara-like mansion outside Nashville.

because he knew how sentimental Dolly is at heart—a realist—but also with a large chunk of sentimentality, and nostalgia for the times, however bad, when she was a kid. That's why the fireplace in the den has a facing of pine logs from the cabin where Dolly was born on Little Pigeon River. When the cabin was torn down, Dolly salvaged a few of the logs.

Despite her love for the house, Dolly insists, "I'm no housekeeper. I don't really like to do that kind of thing." She'd rather spend her time playing horseshoes or tennis, walking around the farm, sometimes doing a bit of gardening with Carl, occasionally helping him tend some of their menagerie of animals. She says she is a real animal lover at heart. And then there are times when she says, "Carl and I could just be sittin' round the house half-naked. That's why we have a house with the land like it has and lots of privacy. I don't want someone bringin' a camera and takin' my picture that way."

Because their home is out of the way, Carl and Dolly don't get bothered much by fans in the tourist buses that go through Nashville. Sometimes a fan will jump over a fence and come into the yard, but Dolly tries to remain philosophical about it. "I don't get bent out of shape about it," she says.

Once a flock of tourists wanted to take some pictures of Dolly's home. But they wanted to make sure that it was okay, so they checked with the man who was working in the yard doing gardening. He told them he thought it would be all right, and after they had finished snapping, they thanked the man and told him they hoped he would not lose his job. The man was Dolly's husband, Carl Dean.

No matter how anyone might regard her unusual marriage, Dolly glows when she talks about this man and her relationship.

"We don't have any problems now at all. Our life is balanced real well. Everything with Carl is as good as it could be."

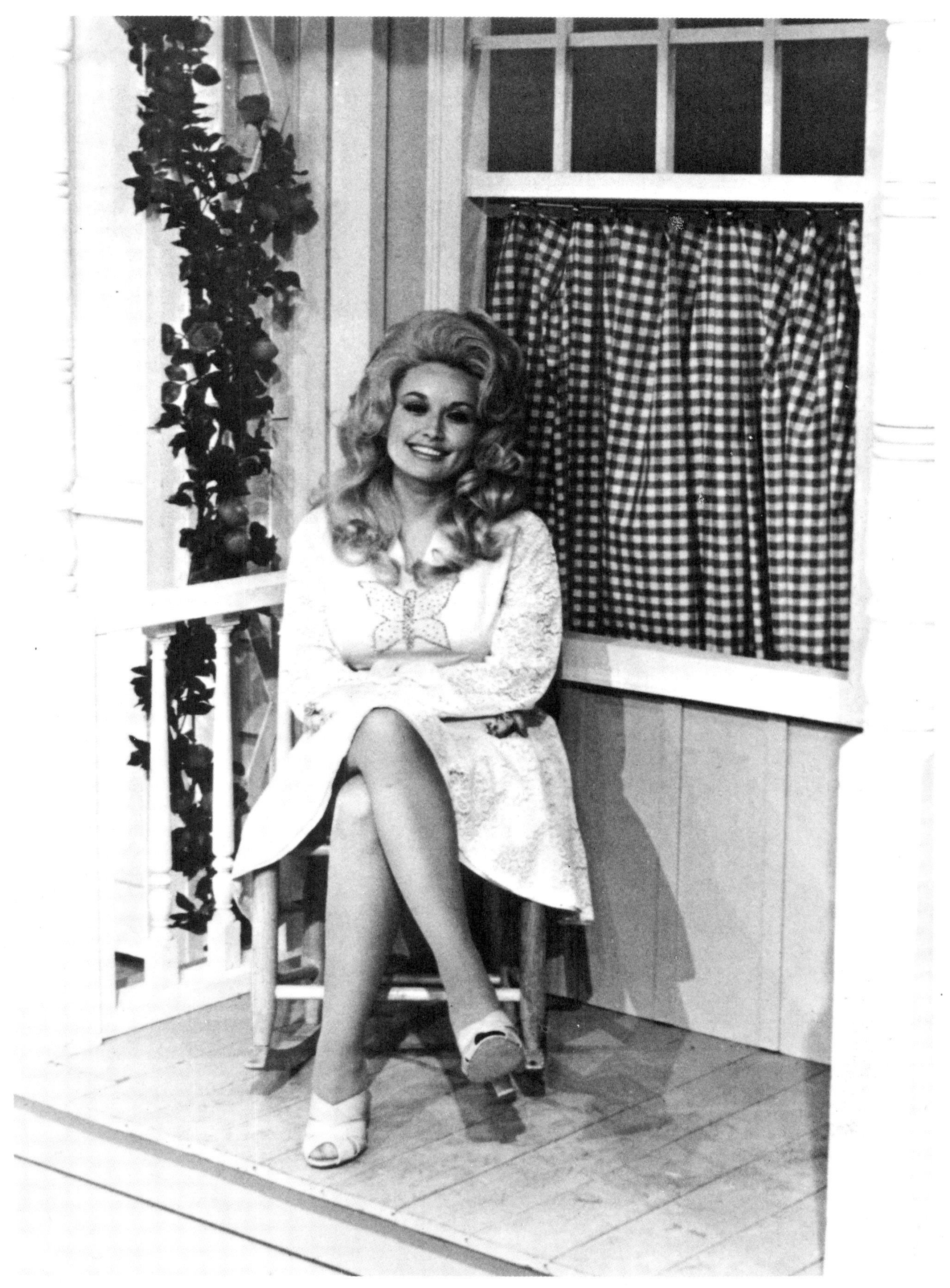

Courtesy of Dolly Parton

A Selective Discography

Albums

All I Can Do - RCA

Award Winners - RCA - featuring "I Will Always Love You"

Bargain Store - RCA - featuring "Bargain Store"

Best of a Great Year - (Vol. 3) - RCA - featuring "My Tennessee Mountain Home"

Best of Chet Atkins and Friends - RCA - featuring "Do I Ever Cross Your Mind"

Best of Dolly Parton - RCA - featuring "Just Because I'm a Woman," "Jolene," "Bargain Store," "Touch Your Woman," "I Will Always Love You," "Love Is Like a Butterfly," "Coat of Many Colors," and "My Tennessee Mountain Home"

Coat of Many Colors - RCA - featuring "Coat of Many Colors"

Dolly - RCA - featuring "The Seeker"

50 Years of Country Music - Camden

Good Old Country Gospel - RCA - featuring "Wings of a Dove"

Great Moments at the Grand Ole Opry - RCA - featuring "Coat of Many Colors"

Heartbreaker - RCA - featuring "Heartbreaker"

Here You Come Again - RCA - featuring "Here You Come Again," "It's All Wrong, but It's All Right," "Me and Little Andy"

I Wish I Felt This Way at Home - Camden - featuring "Just Because I'm a Woman"

In Concert - RCA - featuring "Love Is Like a Butterfly," "Coat of Many Colors," "Bargain Store," and "Roll in My Sweet Baby's Arms" with Ronnie Milsap

In the Beginning - Monument - featuring "Dumb Blonde" and "Something Fishy"

Jolene - RCA - featuring "I Will Always Love You," "Jolene," and "Lonely Comin' Down"

Just the Way I Am - Camden

Love Is Like a Butterfly - RCA - featuring "Love Is Like a Butterfly"

Million Seller Hits Made Famous by America's Country Queens - Alshire

Mine - Camden

My Tennessee Mountain Home - RCA

New Harvest . . . First Gathering - RCA - featuring "Light of a Clear Blue Morning"

Release Me - Powerpak

Stars of the Grand Ole Opry - RCA - featuring "Mule Skinner Blues"

Truck Stop Favorites - Powerpak

20 Great Country Hits - RCA - featuring "Love Is Like a Butterfly" and "Say Forever You'll Be Mine" with Porter Wagoner

Singles

"Bargain Store"/"The Seeker" - RCA

"Coat of Many Colors"/"Touch Your Woman" - RCA

"Dumb Blonde"/"Something Fishy" - Monument

"Heartbreaker" - RCA

"Here You Come Again"/"Me and Little Andy" - RCA

"I Will Always Love You"/"Lonely Comin' Down" RCA

"It's All Wrong, but It's All Right"/"Two Doors Down" - RCA

"Jolene"/"My Tennessee Mountain Home" - RCA

"Joshua"/"Mule Skinner Blues" - RCA

"Just Because I'm a Woman" - RCA

"Light of a Clear Blue Morning"/"There" - RCA

"Love Is Like a Butterfly"/"Sacred Memories" - RCA

"My Blue Ridge Mountain Boy" - RCA

Albums with Porter Wagoner

Best of Porter Wagoner and Dolly Parton - RCA

Porter 'N' Dolly - RCA

Say Forever You'll Be Mine - RCA

20 Great Country Hits - RCA

Singles with Porter Wagoner

"Come to Me"/"If Teardrops Were Pennies" - RCA
"Daddy Was an Old Time Preacher Man"/"Just Someone I Used to Know" - RCA

"How Can I"/"Say Forever You'll Be Mine" - RCA
"We'll Get Ahead Someday" - RCA

Nancy Barr